Saving Jesus

Bhaktivedanta Suddhadvaiti Swami

2021

Title: Saving Jesus

©2021, Guy Bouchié de Belle

Printed in the United States of America

ISBN

ISBN

To my revered spiritual guides,
my beloved students
and all sincere seekers of the Truth

Books by the same author
The science of the guru, guru-tattva
The soul's origins, the Vedic perspective
Search for our meaningful identity, the soul's dharma
If God is one, why are there different religions?
The dynamics of love

Table of contents

Introduction 1

Ch.1. Pauline Christianity, a great, tragic hoax.....11

Ch.2. How reliable are the four Gospels? 41

Ch.3. The Messiah..71

Ch.4. About the "Kingdom of God"............................95

Ch.5. About the resurrection....................................115

Ch.6. About miracles...123

Ch.7. Was Jesus created by the Romans?...............129

Ch.8. Saving the Christians.......................................143

Ch.9. A dark history..163

Ch.10. Yeshua's different roles 173

Ch.11. Why I stopped being a Christian
      but did not become an atheist....................177

Introduction

"Jesus-Christ Superstar, do you think you are what they say you are?"

So much has been written about Jesus. It seems that everyone sees in him what they project on him and want to see in him, whether God Himself as well as His unique son, the universal Savior and the Jewish Messiah, or a prophet, a dissident revolutionary Jew, a rebellious Pharisee, an Essene master, a Stoic, a monistic philosopher, a Buddhist *bodhisattva*, a *guru*, a magician, a liberal, a communist, a socialist, an anarchist, or even a feminist. Western civilization owes much to the events happening between the 1st and 4th centuries, therefore, it seems that nobody can remain indifferent to the character of Jesus. However, there are two Jesus. There is the historical Jesus, the saintly Jew called Yeshua, about whom little of what we know is certain – unless one is a Christian who simply accepts out of faith the Church's version – as contemporary sources do not seem to stand up to present-day scholarly scrutiny (which has also, of course, its limitations). And there is the "official" fabricated Jesus, the Jesus-Christ of ecclesiastical theological faith, the God-human hybrid which was substituted for the historical one, with whom he has very little to do.

Parts of the Christian myth are puzzling and seem irrational, so it is only legitimate to question the superstitions and irrationality surrounding the stories about the beginnings of Christianity. Many great and serious theological thinkers have pondered the same issues; they were not apostates, renegades, or heretics; they were unfailingly devout, reasoned, and highly intelligent thinkers. There were originally the teachings *of* Yeshua, a Jewish spiritual guide and messianic revolutionary who presented a new or updated understanding of the Torah, but they were distorted and replaced by concocted dogmatic teachings *about* Jesus-Christ, which gradually evolved during the first few centuries. Therefore, we ought to "save" Yeshua/Jesus from all the forgeries, myths and meaningless dogmas that have covered him since the early years of "Christianity" and the centuries that followed, as well as from so much speculation about him on the part of various scholars.

Faithful to their monotheistic faith, in the 2nd century B.C. most of the Jews refused with great determination to Hellenize themselves and later Romanize themselves and acknowledge Caesar as their lord and worship him. Yeshua's strongly preaching a deeper commitment to the Torah and the coming of the "Kingdom of God" was his way of resisting Hellenization and Romanization. Israel and Rome were enemies due to that refusal to submit on the part of the Jews. Christianity saw itself quite early as a legitimate competitor of Judaism and a replacement for it. In this respect, anti-Semitism is central to Christianity, which is the first religion in history to have introduced the idea of a religious enemy. Due to the Roman repression of the Jewish revolt of 132-135 CE, Judaism had been driven out of its homeland by the midpoint of the 2nd century; it would never again be a significant threat to what the Romans dared to call the Pax Romana, or Roman "peace" which they established by conquering and subjugating all the people of their empire, the "Barbarians". The Catholic Church became the only official and absolute religious institution of the Roman empire in the 4th century. With the spreading of "orthodox" Christianity, the religion created around Yeshua turned into an imperial tool. Christianity changed the Hebrew concept of "One God," into "One Exclusive Religion," to be imposed on everybody.

To justify its enmity towards the Jews, Trinitarian Christianity had to demonize Judaism and vilify the Jews. A system of doctrinal coercion in opposition to freedom of faith was set up and violently enforced upon the "dissenters" – the members of various communities, sects and factions who had different understandings of Yeshua, his nature and teachings – then upon the masses as well, when political power gave ecclesiastical tyranny the full mechanisms of repression. Thus, for close to 1500 years, the Christian institutions punished, persecuted, tortured and killed anyone who dared to disagree in any way, however small, with the "official" story of Yeshua, witness all the accusations of heresy on other early followers of his teachings. They scapegoated minorities or dissenters, among whom the favorites have been the Jews. They were singled out for persecution by the Roman Catholic Church for refusing to go along with the flow and accept the official Christian accounts and conclusions. The rabbis could not accept the Gospels to be credible reports of the real Yeshua. The Gospel is thus a non-Jewish doctored version of the historical life of Yeshua the Jew, who remained a practicing Jew all his life, and whose original Jewish followers were eventually crushed by their Gentile Christian competitors, and their writings destroyed by said competitors – with the effect if not the purpose of replacing the Jews.

The Church Fathers themselves admitted their difficulties in believing the gospel story of Yeshua, with its mass of impossibilities and contradictions. For instance, while irrationally defending his new faith, former "pagan" Tertullian (160-200AD) acknowledged that the belief that a son of God would take a human birth was "*a shameful thing*"; the belief that he could die was "*monstrously absurd*", and the belief that he rose again after having been buried was "*manifestly impossible*".[1] Towards the end of his life he joined the sect of the Montanists... Augustine himself, who was also a former "pagan" admitted, "*I should not believe in the truth of the Gospels unless the authority of the Catholic Church forces me to do so.*"[2] They were thus confronted with a doctrinal authority, from which their common sense and intellect suffered at first. Unfortunately, they nonetheless upheld it and later reinforced it by their own dogmatic pronouncements.

---

[1] T.W. Doane, *Bible Myths and Their Parallels in Other Religions*, Health Research USA 1985

[2] Rudolph Steiner, *Christianity as mystical Fact*, Anthroposophic Press 1972

There was a marriage of religion and political power in the service of the Roman state, and within this process there was a hijacking of the Hebrew Scriptures to render them null and void, and presenting a new "improved" version (the New Testament) friendly to Roman interests. Actually, the New Testament is primarily a theological document that offers us a limited and obscured historical view of the life of Yeshua. Christian knowledge of Yeshua is contingent on having previously accepted the infallibility of the editors of the Christian Scripture and ecclesiastical authorities. The latter do not need to provide evidence: it is so because it was said that it is so. Only on the basis of this postulate can the faithful accept as truth the Christian version of Yeshua's birth, ministry, trial, crucifixion and resurrection. All of these "facts" are believed with absolute certainty just because they were said to be so by the ultimate authority in Roman Catholicism. Thus Christianity rests on blind faith in dogmas which have actually nothing to do with the teachings of Yeshua but have been gradually created, and which evolved in time. The story of Yeshua' birth, as well as his life and death, would amount to very little unless we accept as an axiomatic truth Paul's myth that "*God sent forth His Son, born of a woman*" (*Galatians* 4:4).

Isn't it quite a paradox? Yeshua presented a message of hope and offered the gift of divine love, which demanded an intense personal commitment but guaranteed an immediate connection with God. Instead, he was monopolized by a hierarchical system of transmission of his distorted, misunderstood teachings, and the personal link to God was fossilized and lost in bureaucratic privileged intermediaries. While he was preaching a personal approach of God untethered by religious hierarchy, and distanced himself from the Jerusalem temple officialdom, making it very evident that salvation and love of God did not depend upon it, a convoluted hierarchical machine with a deplorable dogmatic rigidity was created in his name! He taught to call upon God in the intimacy of one's heart, but big cold buildings were later erected to worship him instead in awe and reverence. God was relegated again to some distant inaccessible figure. Yeshua "*did not have a place where to rest his head*"[3] and spoke of the power of faith, but his so-called representatives created a big corporation and built palaces in which they lived in luxury while cultivating faith in political power.

As it will become clear while reading this book, I subscribe to the following paradigm: Yeshua/Jesus never ceased to be a Jew and never intended to create a new religion. The self-appointed apostle Paul is the one who invented many things about Yeshua and who created a new religion, Christianity, which he preached mainly to the Gentiles. The gospels were written or rather later on edited and adapted to them, especially a Greek and Roman audience. It is a sad paradox since Yeshua's ministry or Messiahship was actually targeted to the Jews, to the deliberate exclusion of the Gentiles, to whom he had apparently no intention to bring his message, as clearly revealed in the following quotes: "*And he said unto them, 'Unto you it is given to know the mystery of the kingdom of God: but unto them that are without, all these things are done in parables: That seeing they may see and not perceive; and hearing they may hear and not understand; lest at any time they should be converted, and their sins should be forgiven them.'*"[4] "*Do not go among the Gentiles...Go rather to the lost sheep of Israel.*"[5] "*I was sent only to the lost sheep of Israel.*"[6] His so-called Great Commission to his disciples to go and teach the gospel to all the nations, found in *Mark* (16:15) and *Matthew* (24:14), is a later interpolation to justify missionary activities among the Gentiles and later on conquests and force conversion. He actually sent them to preach to the lost sheep of Israel in Israel.[7] What a cruel irony that his message

---

[3] Matthew 8:20

[4] Mark 4.11-12

[5] Matthew 10:5-6

[6] Matthew 15:24

destined to his countrymen was deviated and gave birth to anti-Semitism!

A typical Jew of his times

The Gospels describe Yeshua as a typical apocalyptic Jew of his times, born from a Jewish mother, practicing Judaism and addressing the important Jewish issues of his times, a typical Jew who apparently also believed the Jews were God's chosen people and were therefore superior to other peoples. For instance, he is said to have told to a Samaritan woman he met at a well that, *"Salvation comes from the Jews."*[8] Also, he first ignored the Canaanite woman who approached him in the district of Tyra and Sidon and begged him to cure her daughter, but his disciples urged him to send her away, as she kept crying out after them. *"The woman came and knelt before him. 'Lord, help me!' she said. He replied, 'It is not right to take the children's bread and toss it to the little dogs.' 'Yes it is, Lord,' she said. 'Even the little dogs eat the crumbs that fall from their master's table.'"*[9] The reference to the woman and her daughter as dogs implies that they, by birth only, were inferior to the Jews. But why would a *mahatma*, a great soul like Yeshua, behave in such a discriminatory manner? Was this encounter written by the author of *Matthew* with a Jewish audience in mind? Probably as he seems to have been a Jewish Christian addressing Jews after a split with them.

I guess it was hard for the Jews to accept Yeshua's revolutionary teachings like forgiving and even loving one's enemies, since their religious books are full of their deity's statements that he rejoices in killing, warfare, etc. Moreover, they lived according to the Talien law, which prescribes, "one eye for one eye, one tooth

---

[7] Matthew 10:23.

[8] John 4 :22

[9] Matthew 15:21-28

for a tooth", in a society where women were stoned to death for the sin of adultery. Yeshua's mission and desire was to save the people of his land by teaching them to surrender to God and to love Him, but they could not be saved and instead he was crucified, allegedly at the instigation of some of them, apparently the priestly class or Sadducees, not the Pharisees as we have been misled into believing by later editors of the Gospels. Yeshua was born a Jew and followed Judaism. He may have objected to the way in which the Jewish leaders of his day were practicing their faith and were burdening the masses under the law, but he never repudiated Judaism. He never talked about abolishing the Jewish laws, but actually commanded that they be observed even better than by the Pharisees and he showed the example. But he followed them not just for the sake of the law – and he is quoted as having reproached that attitude to those who did – and was therefore accommodating according to time, place and circumstances. He tried to lead people to God through the path of love – which is the basic idea of the practice of *bhakti-yoga*, the essence of the ancient Vedic culture of India – in contrast with the usual Jewish conception that one could not please God without strictly following the 613 *mitzvot* or rules of the Mosaic law. He followed that law but he stressed that its essence was what he called the *"first and great commandment"*[10] which enjoins to *"Love the Lord your God with all your heart, and with all your soul, and with all your strength/mind"* as per *Deuteronomy* (6.4-5). Abraham conceived of Yahweh as an unseen almighty spiritual force lying behind the movements of the universe. The Levites were worshipping Yahweh as one indivisible supreme spirit. Yeshua, however, revealed another nature of God. He pointed to Him as being a loving father, whom he himself addressed as *"abba"*, which means "Dad" in Aramaic. While this is not the highest conception of the Godhead and situates God only in relation to mankind and not God in His own right, so to speak, with His own divine life and activities in His eternal abode – things not known to the Semitic revelation but

---

[10] Mat. 22.35-40

being the specificity of the Vedic one – it made Him much closer and accessible to men than a fearsome distant deity or an impersonal one.

Paul, the upstart

Many modern theologians hold that the teachings of Paul differ markedly from those of Yeshua as found in the gospels.[11] Indeed, a careful analysis shows that Paul greatly differs from Yeshua in terms of the origin of his message, his teachings and his practices.[12] For instance, as noted just above, Yeshua, acknowledging the authority of the Torah, taught to keep the Jewish law to the letter and criticized the Jewish leaders for not doing so. He clearly said that he had not come to abolish the law but to fulfill it, and that not one letter or even one stroke of a letter will pass from it.[13] Why then don't Christians keep the Jewish laws? Simply because Paul claimed that they do not have to. His position is directly contrary to what Yeshua taught! However, Christianity has chosen to follow the easy road concocted by Paul, completely disregarding Yeshua's words. Similarly, nowhere in the Gospels does Yeshua or the writers mention even remotely the Paulinian affirmation that one needs to believe in Yeshua's death and resurrection in order to be forgiven for one's sins and achieve eternal life. It is not believable that Yeshua would not have made it very clear at least once if he had envisioned his own crucifixion as Paul did. Another example is the rich man asking Yeshua what he should do to inherit eternal life, and the disciples asking him who could be saved. Yeshua answered that one should keep the Jewish law, especially the Ten Commandments, sell all that one owns and distribute the money to the poor. Can a Christian dilute Yeshua's words by arguing that his answer only applied during his

---

[11] Hyam Maccoby, *The Mythmaker: Paul and the Invention of Christianity*. Barnes &Nobles, 1986

[12] Wilson Barrie A. *How Jesus Became Christian*. St. Martin's Press. New York. 2008

[13] Mat. 5 :17-18

lifetime but that Paul's ideas hold thereafter? That he is reconciled to God by the crucifixion and the resurrection and that therefore he does not have to worry about whatever Yeshua himself said about eternal life and salvation?[14] One thing is certain, Yeshua's immediate disciples, followers and successors were not Christians. It is quite clear that they kept Judaism as their religion, as opposed to what we have been led over the centuries to believe. Paul's invented religion is completely different from that of Yeshua and his original disciples. Yes, the man on whom the Christian religion is based was actually a member of a different religion, Judaism!

Yeshua and his disciples preached entirely different views than Paul, but those of the self-proclaimed apostle have unfortunately prevailed. Paul had a unique view of Yeshua and he originated a tradition and doctrines that have almost nothing to do with the latter's life, nor the messianic message as it was understood by Yeshua's first followers. Some claim that, due to these differences in teachings, Paul, who literally high-jacked Yeshua's mission, is actually no less than the "second founder" of Christianity, Yeshua being its first.[15] Paul is actually the one and only founder of Christianity as we know it, with its specific doctrines. Indeed, it is a Pauline Christianity that most Christians practice today, and it really developed only when it was officially promulgated as the religion of the Roman empire and enforced with tremendous violence on everyone. Among the critics of Paul was Thomas Jefferson, who wrote that Paul was the *"first corrupter of the doctrines of Jesus."* Other scholars say that Paul's zeal in preaching, which had no equal except his previous zeal to persecute Yeshua's followers – if that story is even true and not a preaching argument meant to convince people that the allegedly

---

[14] Mark Roncace, *Raw Revelation*, ch.4

[15] Dwyer John C. *Church History: Twenty Centuries of Catholic Christianity*, Paulist Press,1985

greatest enemy of the faith had become its most ardent defender – made his particular understanding of Yeshua and his own interpretation of his teachings into a new religion, "Christianity", which he intensely preached; it spread and became the "orthodox" official one, the mighty and fearsome Catholic Church, suppressing the other early currents. It is often said that *"Christianity is a successful cult"*. Maybe we should specify *"Pauline Christianity"* ...

Chapter one

Pauline Christianity, a great, tragic hoax

I stressed in another book – *Search for our meaningful identity* – how knowledge of our spiritual self is crucial to our well-being and happiness. There I mentioned how knowledge of that spiritual self and knowledge about God are inseparable, as the inner self is part and parcel of God and has a very special personal relationship with Him. So we can understand how important it is to have a clear conception of God and as much knowledge about Him as possible. One's beliefs about God are very important as they condition one's whole worldview. I will stress here now the capital importance of religious beliefs by dealing intensively with the fundamental doctrines of Christianity and their consequences. When we read the New Testament, we first have the Gospels, then the Acts of the Apostles, then the Epistles of Paul, then a few more. But in reality, the Epistles, which contain Paul's new Christological "theories" about Yeshua whom he never met in the flesh, are said to have been written first, then the Gospels; the latter were obviously later edited and colored according to Paul's pagan Hellenistic theology of a cosmic dying-and-resurrecting savior-god, inspired from Gnosticism and the mystery cults of his own background, especially *John*. The theories of Paul were already there before the writers of the gospels wrote their accounts and they probably colored their interpretations of Yeshua's activities. We are thus reading texts not just conveying neutral historical and biographical information but documents heavily tinted by religious beliefs. Paul's religion about Christ has actually nothing to do with the teachings of Yeshua the Galilean. We are learning about Yeshua and his first followers not through their personal testimonies but through a biased vision.

I was raised as a Catholic and went to the seminary to study and become a priest. However, unanswered questions made me explore other traditions in search for answers. My quest was oriented to the East by a book on *yoga* which contained some Buddhist philosophy. It answered my most nagging question by making me understand the laws of *karma* and reincarnation. I explored and practiced Tibetan Buddhism, then *kriya-yoga*, and finally came 48 years ago to the path of divine love, *bhakti-yoga*, which is the quintessence of the ancient sacred Vedic literature of India. My knowledge of God has indeed been considerably enriched. When I read again the Bible in the light of the Vedic wisdom, everything is, of course, so much clearer. Moreover, I tasted the sweetness of the path of *bhakti-yoga*, where I learned wonderful, efficient and practical tools to develop my personal relationship with a personal God on the basis of love. I have been frequently asked by Christian friends why I did not go back to the Christian faith of my upbringing once I had learned more about God from the Vedic literature. At the beginning, I did envision myself returning to my original faith with this enriched understanding, full of enthusiasm to share it with my friends, but I was not welcomed when I did, to say the least. Now, after more than four and a half decades of spiritual practices and theological studies, as well as scrutinizing the history of Christianity and its development, I have developed another vision. From the Vedic point of view, Yeshua's status as a *mahatma* or great soul, apparently a somewhat self-realized being, is not seen as unique as it is the goal of life ascribed to all human beings. He is the divine example rather than the divine exception, the son of God as we are all sons of God, rather than the "Only Son of God". I still consider him as my first spiritual master, as he is for so many Westerners who began their spiritual life in the cradle of the Christian faith, but I am not ready to accept blindly anymore what his mission has been turned into, beginning way back with Paul and his "ideas".

A blood line

Some scholars, like Hyam Maccoby[16] or Barrie Wilson, suggest that since just before his departure Yeshua seems to have tacitly accepted the role his disciples gave him – the Messiah – which in those days meant the future king of Israel, it was natural that it would be his blood brother who would lead his followers as something like a prince regent until he came back as he had allegedly announced. While Peter is traditionally presented as the leader of the apostles and the "rock" on which Yeshua built his revolutionary movement, it was actually the eldest of Yeshua's younger siblings, James – called the Just because of his exceeding righteousness in upholding the Law – who led the disciples after the crucifixion. The *Gospel of Thomas* is part of the Nag Hammadi library with about 60 gospels. (It is distinct from the Dead Sea Scrolls, 981 manuscripts discovered in 11 caves from the immediate vicinity of Qumran, an ancient settlement in the West Bank in Israel). This gospel is made up entirely of individual sayings attributed to Yeshua; it confirms James' position as his successor, with Yeshua answering his disciples' enquiry about who will be their leader after his departure, *"No matter where you are, you are to go to James the Just."*[17] In another text, the *Apocryphon*, James speaks of himself as being one of the twelve disciples of his elder brother Yeshua, something covered up in Christianity but acknowledged by Paul himself.[18] In the *Gospel of John*, Yeshua speaks of himself as the "door". In another text found at Nag Hammadi, the *Second Apocalypse of James*, James explains that the "door of Yeshua" means the door to heaven or the door to eternal life. He himself is portrayed as the *"keeper at the door to heaven"* and the *"illuminator and redeemer"*[19] and *"he whom the heavens bless"*. In

---

[16] *The Mythmaker*

[17] Logion 12

[18] Galatians 1:19

[19] SAJ 55.17-18

another passage, James quotes his mother Mary telling him, *"Do not be frightened, my son, because he [Yeshua] said 'My brother' to you. For you were nourished with this same milk. Because of this he [Yeshua] calls me 'My mother'."*[20]

When James was killed in 62 or 69, another blood relative of Yeshua, his cousin Symeon, son of Clopas, a brother of Joseph, occupied his throne, which Eusebius mentioned as having been kept to his days and honored by his successors, and which is said to be preserved in the Armenian cathedral of St James in Jerusalem to this day.[21] It is said that emperor Domitian was searching between 81 and 96 for pretenders to the throne of David and interrogated the grandsons of Jude or Judas Thomas, one of the four brothers of Yeshua, his alleged twin; he did not condemn them as they were poor simple folks. Emperor Trajan, however, crucified Symeon in 100-110 as a Davidic descendent although he was around one hundred and twenty years old.[22] Justus succeeded him. So we are apparently in presence of a messianic dynastic movement within Judaism, not a new religion at all. Its aim was religious but it was expressed in political terms since it saw the religious future of the Jews and of the world as dependent upon Israel's liberation from the Roman yoke. Peter was actually given the keys to the new kingdom as minister, not the keys to the Church, as there was no church and Yeshua did not intend to create one; nor was it the keys to heaven, as the kingdom to come soon was said to be on earth. Everything has been misinterpreted.

It was James the Just, not Peter, who guided the disciples through the young Yeshua movement's first major theological crisis, Paul's misinterpretation of the teachings and mission of Yeshua. James, who could be a bridge between Judaism and its

---

[20] SAJ 50/15-22

[21] Jeffrey J. Butz, *The brother of Jesus and the lost teachings of Christianity*. Inner Traditions. 2005

[22] HE 3.11; 3.19; 3.32

unexpected, paradoxical offshoot, Pauline Christianity, is the most overlooked figure in the history of these early followers. The common teachings of Yeshua are firmly rooted in Hebraic Pharisee tradition. Ecclesiastical authorities have deliberately suppressed James' role, partly due to the dogma of Mary's perpetual virginity which makes Jesus' siblings an embarrassment, and partly in order to minimize the Jewishness of Christianity while emphasizing the theology of Paul. Their theologies are contradictory in many points, with Paul distancing himself from the Jewish roots and thus creating a religion that was not envisioned by Yeshua himself. The Pauline Christian authorities have accused so many early Christianities of being heretical, whereas Pauline Christianity, if one analyses it in an unbiased way, is itself what could be called a Jewish or Judeo-Christian heresy; and as every heresy, it has constructed its identity on the opposition to those who did not accept it. Yeshua's closest followers were then accused of "re-Judaizing", as if they could have so quickly forgotten his reformatory message. How absurd! They were not re-Judaizing, they continued to follow Judaism as he had done! As was James the Just, so was Yeshua: human, typical messianic Jews of their times.

Paul's ideas

Yeshua was allegedly hated by the Jewish religious authorities, the Sadducees, for his successful and charismatic preaching and his having tacitly accepted the title of Messiah, which meant king and implied rebellion against their patrons, the Romans; it was dangerous for the Sadducees for different reasons, among which that they could lose their perks, and repression could come crashing down blindly; it seems that they thought he was particularly dangerous after his allegedly resurrecting Lazarus. When he entered Jerusalem, hailed by his disciples and sitting on an ass's colt as per a biblical prophecy by prophet Zechariah about the Messiah, and committed what would be called now a terrorist act, or at least a political "happening" – opposing the authority of the Sadducees by chasing the merchants and money changers from the precincts of the Jerusalem temple – he, consciously or not, signed his own death warrant and indeed he was crucified within a week. However, Paul unauthorizedly turned the unexpected consequent tragedy of his crucifixion – which put an abrupt halt to his mission after only a short time of preaching – into a voluntary planned sacrifice for the redemption of the sins not only of his disciples or the Jewish nation but of all men.

I am conscious that I am questioning here the basic core of the Christian faith, but let us analyze the facts in an unbiased way. Paul, who is said to have had only a vision of Yeshua once – apparently one year after his resurrection, as he was allegedly on a persecution expedition against the early followers of the Nazarene preacher – proudly claimed that he had understood his message and nature better than his original disciples, with whom he quarreled![23] That is quite a claim, isn't it? He wrote that he had not received any teachings of Yeshua from the apostles or other followers. His personal source of inspiration, he said, was an unmediated revelation not from the pre-resurrection "human" Yeshua but from the post-resurrection "divine" Christ. But Paul's ideas are actually merely his. He was not a legitimate apostle at all, and he created his own brand of religion by usurping and distorting Yeshua's teachings; his epistles contain questionable material.[24]

In spite of the Church painting the image of the earliest followers of Yeshua living all together in total harmony and brotherly love, that early history is actually a black hole and scholars express the opinion that this early following was composed of two main groups who differed in crucial points such as their vision of Yeshua and the way to preach to the Gentiles. Later, other communities centered around different apostles with various

---

[23] *"Paul was in violent opposition to the original 12 Apostles."* (F. C. Baur (1792–1860), professor of theology at Tübingen, Germany)

[24] Robert M. Price. *The Amazing Colossal Apostle, The Search for the Historical Paul*, Signature books, 2012

understandings and leanings emerged. Consequently, the data found in the New Testament is often distorted by various biases and agendas. Indeed, the authors were propagating their personal religious beliefs rather than simply conveying historical information. James the Just was the one who took over for Yeshua, but he lost out to Paul in the battle for what the aftermath of Yeshua would become. James and Paul did not see eye to eye on things. Paul introduced himself in Galatians 2 as: *"Paul, an apostle sent neither by human commission nor from human authorities but through Jesus the Christ and God the Father"*. He criticized *"those who were supposed to be acknowledged leaders – what they actually were makes no difference to me – contributed nothing to me"* and named James as one of these pillars. There were big differences between them on ideological grounds. Paul's interpretations, which became the foundation of the Christian Church, are in many ways its betrayal.[25]

The closest followers of Yeshua were disillusioned by the crucifixion because it was not an expected outcome of his mission. After all, he had just been defeated by the very forces they thought he intended to overcome. As the gospels have been completely re-written to fit Paul's interpretations, it is very difficult to know the truth. Is it possible that Yeshua expected to have to go up to death to bring about the "Kingdom of God"? He allegedly thought it would be ushered by John the Baptist's preaching and baptizing, his own preaching and that of his disciples; he had sent them all over the country to tell people to repent of their sins and amend their ways in order to bring about that Kingdom then enter into it. Although it has been claimed that he had come to Jerusalem ready to give his life to "save" his countrymen by forcing God's hand so that He would bring in the "Kingdom"[26], as I wrote in another book – *If God is*

---

[25] *The brother of Jesus and the lost teachings of Christianity*.

[26] Albert Schweitzer, *The Quest for the Historical Jesus*, 1906, published by Macmillan, NY, in 1968

one, why are there many religions? – as per another prophecy of Zechariah he nonetheless seemed to have been expecting that a miracle would happen on the Mount Olivet when the High Priest's soldiers came to arrest him. After the crucifixion, his followers apparently viewed the empty tomb as evidence that God had resurrected him into heaven. With their belief in such a resurrection, they were refocused to continue to follow his teachings and, we are told, to expect a quick fulfillment. Were they really expecting him to quickly come down from heaven to resume his earthly mission and rule the earth? And did they think this was imminent?

In contrast, instead of the Jewish concept of a human messiah reigning over a restored kingdom of Israel having become the new center of the world, Paul invented a divine cosmic figure, Christ, and envisioned the kingdom as open to all peoples with admittance predicated simply on accepting Christ as a personal savior, and without any obligation to perform good works. Paul relegated positive action to a secondary position, *"For by grace you have been saved through faith; and that not of yourselves, it is the gift of God; not as a result of works, so that no one may boast."*[27], contrary to the teachings of Yeshua. However, it is doubtful that God favors faith over acts of love, and the opposite message is indeed presented in *James*, who insisted that religious faith should be exemplified by action, otherwise that religion was deceptive and futile, a sham: *"What use is it, my brethren, if someone says he has faith but he has no works? Can that faith save him? If a brother or sister is without clothing and in need of daily food, and one of you says to them, 'Go in peace, be warmed and be filled,' and yet you do not give them what is necessary for their body, what use is that? Even so faith, if it has no works, is dead, being by itself."* (2.14-17) Union with God, to which thoughtful Christians hold that Jesus-Christ invited man, requires not just faith, but correct practice of faith. The importance of *praxis*, in the sense of action, is indicated in the dictum of Maximus the Confessor (580-662) in no uncertain terms: *"Theology without action is the theology of demons."*

---

[27] *Eph.* 2.8-9

The *Book of Acts* appears to be partly the work of a revisionist with an agenda. It contains a propaganda exercise intended to fictitiously portray unity in the early Church. It is using the Yeshua movement to gain legitimacy for Paul's new one, grafting his non-Jewish offshoot on to Judaism, thereby giving it an ancient venerable pedigree, which was important and needed for proselytizing to Gentiles. It is trying to obscure the fact that Paul's movement originated only with him, not at all with Jesus. Contrary to what Luke writes and wants people to believe, Paul was never directly affiliated to the Jewish Yeshua community of Jerusalem, the Nazarenes. He had started his own movement completely independently from them, after having supposedly changed his mind about Jesus and his following. Among various devices, Luke is trying to provide a link between Paul and Yeshua and his movement by depoliticizing the trial of Stephen – the first so-called "Christian" martyr and in reality probably an activist and militant of Yeshua's Jewish movement – and remodeling it as a religious trial, just like it was done for Yeshua's. A thorough examination of that fictional muddled story shows inconsistencies. *Acts* has Stephen being accused of blasphemy for statements which were not blasphemous at all, and words are attributed to him which belong to Paul's philosophy *after* his conversion, whereas at that time Paul was present and participated directly in the assassination of Stephen – although *Acts* tries to minimize his role, saying Paul was a youth who just looked after the clothes of the killers. Actually, Paul could not have been a youth since *Acts* describes him right after that as harrying the church and seizing men and women and sending them to prison!

Acts then has Paul going to Damascus with letters from the High Priest to the synagogues authorizing him to arrest Christians and bring them back to Jerusalem. This could not be true either, as the High Priest had no such authority on synagogues but only on the Temple, what to speak out of Judea in a foreign country! If Paul was ever sent to Damascus by the High Priest, it could only have been as an undercover agent entrusted with a clandestine mission to kidnap some leading Nazarenes who had fled there – some say Peter himself, or maybe even Yeshua who had survived crucifixion – and bring them back illegally with the help of some mercenaries. *Acts* has Paul preaching to the Jews of Damascus after his existential crisis and alleged vision on the road to Damascus, maybe a frontal lobe seizure, infuriating them to the point that they wanted to kill him – another vilification of the Jews as villains – and them watching the gates of the city day and night in order to murder him. In contrast, Paul wrote in *Corinthians* (11:32) that it was the governor under the local king who was trying to arrest him. *Acts* gives three contradictory accounts of what happened to Paul, all different from Paul's own narration of it in *Galatians*. Does this not betray a personal agenda? *Acts* has Paul being converted and baptized in Damascus and going to Jerusalem right after, then participating in the preaching there in a subordinate role as a new convert, whereas Paul writes in the same *Epistle to the Galatians* that he did not speak to anyone about what happened to him, did not go to Jerusalem to consult with the apostles but went to Arabia – like Moses after receiving the tables of the law – and then back to Damascus...

Is it possible that it dawned on Paul what a great career he could make for himself by creating his own movement through high-jacking Judaism and the particular teachings of Yeshua the Jew? He stated that he was not converted but claimed that what he preached was the proper understanding of what ancient Judaism had always been about; that it had not been taught to him by any man but that he had received it directly from Yeshua the Christ through a revelation, which surpassed the direct disciples' and which he claimed was followed by other visions and revelations. So it should be clearly understood that what he taught was not some existing form of Christianity to which he was converted. He did not even spread a new version of Yeshua's teachings different from his direct followers. He actually never spoke about Yeshua's life and never cared to quote any of his teachings. He only cared about his own. He created a completely new religion born from his alleged revelation. *Acts* was written decades after Paul's Epistles. Things had changed a lot in the meanwhile. Paul's ideas had become the basis of a new religion, Christianity, but its leaders were trying to make it appear that there had never been any rift between Paul and the Jerusalem disciples, that they had all believed like him in a divine Yeshua and in his sacrificing himself for the sins of all mankind. A myth of unity between them was being built.

In reality, Paul's alleged vision was what initiated Christianity, just as Yahweh's appearance in the burning bush is what had initiated Judaism. His new religion was very far-removed from Judaism, however, which was still followed by Yeshua's original followers and closest disciples, the Nazarenes. Their particular brand of Judaism later became known as the Ebionite sect (from the Hebrew word '*evyonim*' meaning 'poor men') when they divided; their mood was the closest to Yeshua's, so much more than the official Church based not on Yeshua's teachings but on Paul's concoctions. Being persecuted and rejected by the orthodoxy of both Christianity and Judaism who considered them heretical,[28] the Ebionites gradually split into various groups, some combining Gnostic elements, and they faded into history around the 10th century. Their correct, unfiltered view of Yeshua are expressed in the Koran by Muhammad, whom they have apparently influenced. They considered Yeshua as both a prophet and the Messiah who would usher in the "Kingdom of God" on earth and would reign on it. They thought that his message had been perverted by Paul, whom they deemed a false apostle. They wrote that Paul was actually a Greek who went to Jerusalem and became passionately attracted to the daughter of the High Priest and therefore converted in order to marry her; upon not being accepted, out of frustration he started his own religious movement in opposition to the Torah. In another document, they accuse him of having shunned the observance of the Torah mainly in order to obtain the backing of the Romans

---

[28] Jerome wrote about them to Augustine in the beginning of the 4th century, "*They want to be both Jews and Christians but they are actually neither. They want to be Jews because they scrupulously follow the Jewish traditions, but they are not because they accept the Messiah rejected by the Jews and are therefore also rejected by them. They want to be Christians because they recognize Christ as the Messiah, but they are not accepted as such because, considering him as mere prophet, they don't recognize his divinity. They are therefore also rejected by the Christians. They have then developed an identity based on opposition to those who have rejected them.*"

for his own self-aggrandizement. They even hold him responsible for having inflamed the Romans against the Jews by his heavy anti-Jewish propaganda and thus brought about the attack and destruction of Jerusalem and the temple. Maccoby holds that the Ebionites had a profound underground influence on Christianity and represented an alternative tradition in it that never quite died out.

Paul insisting in *Galatians* that he had learned nothing from men, that his knowledge of Jesus-Christ came from his personal revelation and realization, that *"God had set me apart from birth and called me through his grace, chose to reveal his son to me and **in me**, in order that I might proclaim him among the Gentiles"* is another big claim, isn't it? By writing, "***in me***", he is actually stating more or less directly that he is higher than all the prophets and patriarchs including Moses; he claims to embody divine power. In *How Jesus became a Christian,* p 109, Barrie Wilson calls *Galatians* a bombshell. Paul's megalomania transpires in other letters. He claims in *Corinthians* 12 to have had supremely mystical experiences, to have been caught up into "the 3rd heaven" and in "paradise" and to have heard words so secret that no human lips may repeat them, and elsewhere to have special marks or stigmata on his body, showing the depth of his self-identification with the sufferings of Yeshua on the cross, a conception foreign to Judaism and Jesus' authentic followers, but traceable to Gnosticism or/and mystery cults where one identified with the god.

Acts is playing another number to try to link Yeshua and the Pauline Church. It tells of Peter having a dream where he is repeatedly told in spite of his protests to eat food considered unclean according to Judaism, with the remark that, *"it is not up to him to call profane what God counts clean"*; then of his visiting a Roman centurion and his entourage and telling them that he was shown that there are no profane or unclean men, then eating with them, preaching to them and the Holy Spirit descending upon them, then Peter baptizing them "in the name of Jesus-Christ". Then when Peter goes back to Jerusalem, he is criticized by Yeshua's other followers but after telling them of his dream all are convinced that he did good. Thus *Acts* is trying to disguise the deep gulf between Peter and Paul's respective groups – a Jewish one and a "Christian" one – and Peter allegedly moving towards a Pauline position. At the same time, under the cover of a symbolic dream where unclean food stands for unclean people and the idea that Gentiles should be admitted to the Yeshua movement without having to convert first to Judaism, it is hinted that the whole distinction between Jews and Gentiles should be given up and that the Jewish concept of purity based on the Torah should be also done with, as well as the Torah itself, as per Paul. Thus *Acts* has the whole Jerusalem Yeshua movement headed by Peter (and not by James) "divinely" guided towards a Pauline position. In other words, the movement of Yeshua within Judaism with a special belief in Yeshua as the long expected Messiah who died, resurrected and is soon coming back, is being painted in "Pauline colors" by *Acts*, which tries to blur its difference with Paul's new religion and to recuperate it. Under this attempt, Peter and Paul will later be depicted as twin saints, brothers in the faith.

According to the same *Acts*, however, there was a controversy between the Jerusalem group that maintained a commitment to Jewish law as a condition for accepting non-Jewish proselytes – a proof that they remained strict Jews and were never "Christians" – and Paul's approach that rejected it in favor of admitting more proselytes, not to Judaism obviously but to his new "religion". The issue of circumcision as part of the conversion process was central to this controversy. Most of these proselytes came from the unlettered masses and the "God-fearing" Gentiles, people who were attracted to Judaism and attended the synagogue but were not ready to convert and accept all what it implied, especially circumcision as adults. It makes sense how a pseudo-Judaism (i.e. Christianity) without a circumcision requirement would have been more appealing to non-Jews. And as Paul and his successors' target audience shifted from Jews to Gentiles, they shifted the emphasis in their message from promoting Yeshua as the Messiah to the Jews, to promoting him to the Gentiles as the Savior from their sins who would take them to the "Kingdom of God", accessible without full observance of the Mosaic law.

Luke narrates in *Acts* a Jerusalem conference (pompously dubbed later the first "apostolic council") where Paul was summoned to answer to accusations of deviationism, because some preachers had come from Jerusalem to Antiochus and found out that Paul was not telling his congregation of new Gentile converts about their need to be circumcised and follow the Torah. This in itself is another undeniable proof that Yeshua's disciples and followers continued to practice Judaism like he did himself throughout his own life and that Paul unauthorizedly started his own concocted "religion". After a long debate, Peter is reported to have made a speech and *Acts* puts in his mouth Pauline arguments, considered blasphemous by Jews, making him say that he thinks, *"that we should not lay on the shoulders of these converts a yoke which neither we nor our fathers were able to bear, that it is by the grace of the Lord Jesus that we are saved and so are they."* Then James is said to conclude by confirming Peter's idea of not imposing to the new Gentile converts to follow the Mosaic laws laid in the Torah and suggesting that they should be instructed by letters to simply follow four regulations similar to four out of the seven Noahide laws.[29] This is obviously a concoction. It does not make any sense since they were not converting in the opinion of James to anything else but to Judaism. Paul came back from the meeting with his own understanding of it, but especially with his purposes confirmed: he was allegedly given the green light to preach to the Gentiles without imposing the Torah to them – a Torah that he was obsessed with and personally considered as obsolete and unnecessary although he did not reveal that opinion to the Apostles. The author of *Acts* is taking his readers for another ride as Paul gives his own version of the whole story in *Galatians*. He does not say he was summoned by his seniors but that he was "divinely inspired" to go. He claims that he openly revealed his new doctrines in private to them, turning what was actually maybe his trial into a colloquy between equal

---

[29] They are: Do not deny God. Do not blaspheme God. Do not kill. Do not engage in illicit sexual relations. Do not steal. Do not eat the blood of animals. Establish courts to ensure obedience to the law.

leaders: *"But the men of high reputation (not that their importance matters to me: God doesn't recognize these personal distinctions) did not prolong the consultation, but on the contrary acknowledged that I had been entrusted with the Gospel for gentiles as surely as Peter had been entrusted with the Gospel for Jews. For God whose action made Peter an apostle to the Jews also made me an apostle to the Gentiles. Recognizing the favor thus bestowed upon me, these reputed pillars of our society, James, Peter and John, accepted Barnabas and myself as partners and shook hands upon it, agreeing that we should go to the Gentiles while they went to the Jews. All that was asked was that we should keep their poor in mind, which was the very thing I made it my business to do* (2:6-10)." In plain language, this is called whitewashing the facts and making false claims.

Later on, Peter visited Antiochus and sat and ate with the Gentile converts, thinking that they were following the directives given in the Jerusalem meeting; then, as information had reached James that Paul had not transmitted to his congregation those directives – some scholars say that he was unaware of them (!?) others that this meeting never took place and is a literary device of Luke – emissaries came to Antiochus and warned Peter about it, upon which Peter withdrew and broke away from Paul. In the following years, there were more emissaries sent from Jerusalem to counteract Paul's teaching about the abrogation of the Torah – emissaries Paul abuses in his Epistles – until he was summoned again to answer the serious charge that he was preaching not only to his new Gentile converts but also to the Jews of the *diaspora* that they did not need to follow Moses's law, another crystal-clear proof that the Jerusalem followers of Yeshua remained Jews and viewed Paul's teachings as deviant or heretical. Paul answered the accusation deceptively, denying what he was actually doing. The leaders among the apostles then put him to test, ordering him to dissipate the doubts of the Jerusalem movement by publicly going through a ritual of purification with a group of four men and paying for their expenses. Paul did so, but was seen by a group of Jews from Asia Minor who started a riot against him, accusing him of teaching people...to give up the Torah! Paul was saved by the Roman police, which later was about to flog him when he declared that he was actually a Roman citizen! To the commandant who told him that it had costed him a lot of money to acquire this citizenship, he answered that it was his from birth, although there is good reason to believe that he had actually recently obtained it by using some of the big sum of money he had collected from his congregation and brought to Jerusalem...

Paul was brought to the Sanhedrin where the High Priest accused him. Paul cleverly played the Pharisees against the Sadducees, claiming to be a Pharisee himself, and had the Pharisee defend him. Maccoby underlines that this incident gives further support to the picture of the Pharisees not being opposed to Yeshua's movement but defending its members, as well as the fact that it was the Pauline movement which blackened the reputation of the Pharisees by distorting their image in the New Testament, which is mostly a Pauline scripture. As the High Priest was not willing to let Paul go scot free, he planned to send his crew of ruffians to assassinate him. Paul was informed of the plot by his nephew and required the commandant to remove him to Caesarea. However, the High Priest came there after a few days and accused Paul in front of the Governor, who did not however hand him over to him, probably expecting some substantial bribe. Two years later, when a new governor arrived, the High Priest renewed his accusation, at which time Paul appealed for a trial in Rome before Caesar as a Roman citizen; he journeyed there and allegedly was martyred as well as Peter during Nero's persecution in 64. Legend has it that milk and not blood flowed from his decapitated head...When Paul was in prison in Rome, he was writing to the various communities that he had founded, claiming deceptively that it was for the sake of preaching the gospel that he was imprisoned.

The Jews do not take the Torah literally. They have a tradition of interpreting it in various ways, *midrash*. Paul reinterpreted ancient Biblical stories and the 127 messianic prophecies of the Torah in this *midrash* fashion, in the light of a metaphysical, archetypal "Christ" or Messiah (*'Christos'* in Greek). Actually, these Biblical predictions were to encourage the exiled enslaved

Jews, to solace them and give them hope for a Messiah who would free them from the yoke of their oppressors. That Messiah is presented as an earthly leader, a powerful king, but in Isaiah there is a mention of a "suffering servant" to whom the Jews could identify. Paul and his followers twisted the predictions and applied them to Jesus-Christ, stressing the passage of Isaiah's suffering servant, with whom some scholars say that Yeshua seems to have identified towards the end of his ministry. Paul definitely broke away from Judaism and inaugurated a distinct religion when he created the new ritual of Eucharist as the basic sacrament of Christianity, founded on a special revelation he claimed to have had. But, although there was a last supper, during which Yeshua distributed consecrated food to his disciples to confirm their being eligible to enter into the "Kingdom of God" – copied from Paul by the Gospel writers – how is it that this was not observed by the Jerusalem Yeshua movement as a new sacrament, as confirmed in *Acts* 2:42, which simply states that they were breaking bread like all Jews did and still do, without giving it any mystical significance?! Its basis is not Judaism nor Yeshua himself as usually thought but pagan mystery cults, where there is an identification with the deity, who grants salvation through the faithful's mystical sharing of his death and resurrection. Paul was not a theologian but a mythologist.

Yeshua played a role in Judaism, an already existing religion, whereas Paul made him the fictional founder of a new one! He portrayed him as a Gnostic-like descending divine savior by whom one can only be rescued from the world of evil, and this simply by having faith in him and entirely relying on him, not by following the Torah, which, by the way, he said was authored by angels and not by God. He asserted that the main prophets of the Bible were in fact proto-Christians who had never regarded the Torah as anything more than temporarily binding in the expectation of the Messiah who would abrogate it. Paul claimed that the path of salvation was through faith, not Torah observance. He very selectively quoted *Genesis* which states that

Abraham had faith in God and was therefore considered righteous, thus ignoring the whole history of Judaism between Moses to whom the Torah was revealed and the period in which he lived himself. He thus misapplied several texts, hijacking the whole biblical narrative as well as the Yeshua character and appropriated them, utilizing them by injecting into them his own concocted interpretations, thus creating a counterfeit religion. In stark contrast with Judaism, which is a down to earth tradition aiming at transforming the world by strictly following the Torah and not being "saved" and escaping from it, Paul embraced the Gnostic vision that the human condition is helpless. He said that the Torah is not teaching men how to behave but is showing them that they are hopeless in trying to follow its injunctions and that they need to acquire another nature, a spiritual one (pneumatic) by salvation; that salvation does not come from sacred knowledge, *gnosis*, as per the Gnostics, but from simply believing in Christ, the savior that came from the world above. He thus divinized a man, Yeshua, turning the not divine into a deity, which is the definition of idolatry. The Jews, on the other hand, never said that there was the need for a Messiah for the redemption of souls, as they hold that observers of the rules and regulations of the Torah in every generation achieve salvation in the afterlife without a Messiah. The French Jew Salvator wrote in 1838 that, *"Jesus was the last representative of a mysticism which, drawing its nutriment from the other oriental religions, was to be traced among the Jews from the time of Solomon onwards. In Jesus, this mysticism allied itself with Messianic enthusiasm."* According to the German Scholar Friedrich W. Ghillany, writing in 1864, *"The worship offered to Jesus after his death by the Christian community is also not derived from pure Judaism but from a Judaism influenced by oriental religions. The influence of the cult of Mithra, for instance, is unmistakable. The idea of eating and drinking the flesh and blood of Jesus, which is operative in the Last Supper, would be inexplicable without that influence. The whole Eastern world was at that time impregnated with Gnostic ideas, which centered in the revelation of the Divine in the human. Christianity itself is a kind of Gnosis. Jesus' teaching, however, is Rabbinic; all his ideas, like the theme of the need for repentance, have their source in the Judaism of his times, the world of thought of which we can reconstruct from the Rabbinic writings."*

In the 16th and last chapter of his amazing book, Maccoby is masterfully demonstrating how Paul indeed took various elements already existing in Judaism, Gnosticism and pagan mystery religions and combined them in a unique creative way. This speculative combination is what made Pauline Christianity so unique and also what made it rejected by the Jews, including Yeshua's original followers, as well as by the Gnostics, and only attracted the Gentiles or so-called pagans, who saw in it some familiar elements. Neither the Jews nor the Gnostics could accept it as it was incorporating an element which was repugnant to them: the human sacrifice element. It was foreign and abhorrent to the Jews since centuries. As far as the Gnostics who were attracted to Christianity are concerned, they did not see Christ as sacrificing himself since, in their dualist view of matter and spirit being totally opposed, they thought he only had the appearance of a human being and therefore did not die on the cross – a conception considered by the Catholics to be a heresy called Docetism or "appearing like". They saw him as revealing *gnosis*, the secret knowledge needed to attain salvation from the dark forces imprisoning the soul in matter. That is also why the Gnostic Christian groups, although very influential in early Christianity, were considered heretical because they could not and did not accept that sacrificial aspect of the Pauline cult, which demanded Christ to be tortured, shed blood and agonize as in the gory Attis mystery cult, so that sinful mankind could be redeemed from doom.

Now, let us see what were Paul' alleged "revelations" and "realizations". He had quite simple but quite appealing arguments for preaching: "Man, in the form of Adam and Eve, was originally perfect and immortal, but his sin of disobedience to God made him a mortal being, as death is the salary of sin. All men carry that original stigma, but Jesus the Christ, the long expected Messiah, came and died on the cross to save everyone from that original sin. As one man, Adam, is the original cause of sin,[30]one man, Jesus-Christ, is the cause of freedom from sin as he died on the cross for the sins of all men including yours.[31]He resurrected, defeating death, not only for himself but for everyone. So you can also escape death by simply accepting him as your savior. Apocalypses is near. Christ is coming back very soon." This message of hope was very appealing in a society obsessed by the law and the fear of sinful reactions after death, as well as oppressed by the Roman yoke, so it was welcomed by many simple folks, hardly by the intelligent class, especially when it spread beyond Israel. By and large, the early Christians were mainly illiterate and uncultured, described as "the scum of society and slaves". Christianity did not compete for these people with the Roman thinkers, but with the mystery religions, as both have irrational elements which were of much appeal to such a group of people. Most apparently believed they would see the return of Jesus-Christ in their own lifetime. However, upon analyzing Paul's seemingly sound and logical arguments in their biblical context, we can detect an elaborate construction. Let us go through them.

First, Paul stated that Adam and Eve were created perfect and immortal. Where exactly does the Torah (re-baptized "the Old Testament") say that? And where does it openly teach that the soul is created? Actually, the souls are not created but eternal and our presence in this world is not due to God creating us here but to our falling from a higher stratum because we misused our free will, as taught through the myth of Adam and Eve. But even if we take this allegorical story in a literal way, Paul's statement that they were perfect and immortal is not supported in any way by the Old Testament. Being endowed with free will – which is

---

[30] *"Sin came into the world through one man,"* and *"by the one man's disobedience the many were made sinners"*. *(Romans 5:12,19)*.

[31] *"For since death came by man, the resurrection of the dead came also by man. For as in Adam all die, even so all shall be made alive in Christ."* (I Corinthians 15:21-22).

inseparable from consciousness itself and carries the possibility of doing something else than God's will – they disobeyed and ate of the fruit of the tree of knowledge; then they were exiled before they could eat of the fruit of another tree, the tree of life, which would make them immortal (*Gen.* 3:22). So it means that they were created mortal![32] Second, Paul claimed that Adam and Eve sinned by eating a fruit of the first tree. Again it contradicts the Old Testament which does not say that they sinned, but that they disobeyed. The word 'sin' is mentioned later for the first time in the Old Testament, when Cain killed his brother Abel. Third, Paul stated that *"the wages of sin is death"*,[33] another conception foreign to the Old Testament which speaks of personal atonement sacrifices and repentance. From a psychological point of view, it could be said that he introduced the fear element, considered vital in controlling people.

Fourth, Paul invented the transmission of the so-called "Original Sin" of Adam and Eve to all their descendants – every human being – through sexuality. This fourth element is foreign to Judaism and not supported by the Old Testament, which is originally a Jewish scripture. How come the Jews did not have a conception of an "Original Sin" for over one thousand years? Although it is not in the Old Testament, Paul pulled it off and it passed unchallenged as a genuine teaching, which was adopted and developed by Justin Martyr (c 100-165). Augustine (354-430), considered the first great Christian theologian, unfortunately accepted this myth and established it as dogma. Fifth, having invented a so-called sin and thus created the need for a savior, Paul then revealed the goal of his scheme: he

---

[32] It may be inspired by *The Book of the Cow of Heaven*, an old Egyptian text, which describes a fracture in the original unity of creation as the reason for the suffering found in the world: Men rebelled and plotted against the supreme Lord, Ra. He punished them through his "violent eye", the goddess Hathor, who started to slaughter them and thus brought death into the world.
[33] *Romans* 6.23

claimed that Yeshua willingly died to save men from their sin. He gave this hope to the people, and he elaborated, stressing a near Apocalypses. He dismissed the value of following the Mosaic Law of the Torah, claiming that since Yeshua's sacrifice people were not any longer under that law but under "grace", accessible through mere faith in Yeshua. In a very crafty and devious way, he thus perverted the original teachings of Judaism, as well as Yeshua's message, which was rooted in Judaism, claiming he could offer his followers all the benefits of Judaism while bypassing all its requirements. That made his new cult, a thoroughly Hellenized one, very appealing as it was much easier to join and follow.

By reviewing Paul's first four arguments which are all false, we can deconstruct his faulty theology. Indeed, the Fall of Man from Eden and the concomitant "Original sin" and the Atonement of Sin by Yeshua are the cardinal doctrines of Christianity. Belief in the Atonement is linked with belief in the Fall from Eden. They are inseparable dogmas. If there was no Fall, no "Original Sin", the need for the Atonement disappears, as well as the necessity of a Redeemer. Paul invented the highly speculative and heretical idea that God had taken a human body of flesh and bones in the form of Jesus the Christ, and died. In reality, God never takes a material body when He comes down in this world, just like the director of a jail does not need to put on a prisoner's dress to visit that jail. This fabrication of Paul is considered blasphemous by the followers of Vedic culture, by the Jews, by many early Christians, and later by the Muslims, who have long believed that Paul purposefully corrupted the original revealed teachings of Yeshua[34] by making Christianity into a theology of the cross and introducing the Original Sin and the need for redemption. In

---

[34] Ed Hindson; Ergun Caner, *The Popular Encyclopedia of Apologetics: Surveying the Evidence for the Truth of Christianity.* Harvest House Publishers.2008, p. 280.

Sunni polemics, Paul is said to have played the role of deliberately corrupting the early teachings of Yeshua.[35]

A clear departure from the understanding of the first disciples

No one in the original group of Yeshua's Jewish followers viewed him as being divine. They did not believe he was God incarnate, which would be unquestionably contrary to their Jewish faith, but rather as their rabbi, their spiritual guide, at best as a prophet setting the stage for the coming of the new kingdom of Israel which was dreamed to be reestablished on earth. After apparently seeing him again after his death by crucifixion – or what they believed was his death – his subsequent burial and what they believed was his resurrection, these Jewish followers of Yeshua considered him divine, but in a way very different from the divine-human Christology that evolved later, in the wake of Paul's Hellenistic, divinizing doctrine. What they meant by that was not at all what people mean today. *Apotheosis* refers to the idea that an individual has been raised to godlike stature. Indeed, the Greeks believed since a long time that an exceptional man could be resurrected as a god after his death. From at least the ninth century BCE, the long-deceased heroes linked with founding myths of Greek sites were accorded rites in their "hero-temple". The Macedonian kings were later worshipped in Greek Asia; such Hellenistic state leaders could be raised to a status equal to the gods before death (e.g. Alexander the Great) or afterwards. The custom passed to the Roman emperors, which became seen as being divine and had a cult attached to their persons. 36 out of 60 between Augustus and Constantine were apotheosized. Julius Caesar claimed to have descended from Venus. Titus established an imperial cult for his father Vespasian, secured the deification of his sister Domitillia and linked himself with Jupiter, claiming that the god had mandated

---

[35] Ross Brann, *Power in the Portrayal: Representations of Jews and Muslims in Eleventh- and Twelfth-Century Islamic Spain*. Princeton University Press. 2009, pp. 65–6.

his rule. He received the title of Pontifex Maximus, which made him the official head of all the priests of Rome.

The more divine the emperor in his subjects' opinion, the better for him as it was easier to control and manipulate them. Domitian deified his brother Titus after his death. His obsession with his own divinity was well-known. The recently-deceased emperor would receive a divine body instead of his physical one, which would disappear. Trustworthy citizens would witness the prodigy. Thus, in a story similar to the Gospel appearances of the resurrected Yeshua and the commissioning of the disciples, Romulus, the founder of Rome, descended from the sky to command a witness to bear a message to the Romans regarding the city's greatness, *"Declare to the Romans the will of Heaven that my Rome shall be the capital of the world."* He was then taken up on a cloud…In this Hellenistic perspective, Yeshua's body disappeared after his crucifixion and burial. The tomb was found empty, but he then allegedly reappeared in an immortalized body like a god, then ascended to heaven. The author of *Mark*, a Pauline Christian, spoke for his Gentile audience of Yeshua as "Son of God", a divine being whose suffering, death and resurrection were essential to God's plan for redemption. The author of *Matthew* later presented Yeshua's appearance in Galilee (28:19-20) as a Greco-Roman *apotheosis*: his human body had been transformed so he could ascend to heaven. The synoptic gospels grant the highest status to Yeshua. Paul had gone further and described him as one with the Godhead, but not fully clearly, probably due to some scruples given the Jewish commitment to monotheism. The author of John crossed that step. Traditional mainstream Christian theology, both East and West, now views Yeshua as the preexisting God who undertook mortal existence and not as a mortal being who attained divinity. But, I repeat, it is not what the original disciples believed during Yeshua's lifetime, and it is not what he claimed about himself. It is an idea which evolved and looked very different in the fourth century than it did in the first. How did Yeshua become God? The real answer to this question is found centuries later in the numerous Synods, Councils, controversies, and debates concerning the precise nature of the Christ, determined not by God, but by mere mortals in committee![36]

Beliefs have consequences and, although religious faith is indeed admirable, the value of faith is according to what or whom one believes. To believe that a holy man is God implies that you do not need to develop your relationship with God Himself, especially hum-bogged as He is in a mysterious Trinity – the only accessible and therefore only truly significant member of which is that holy man turned into "the only Son" equal to God. Therefore, Christianity is not linking people with God but with Jesus-Christ. It is exclusively focused on his person. The Christians always speak of committing to him, of developing their relationship with him, never with God, who is simply invoked ritualistically in the prayer, "*Our father who are in heaven...*" But God desires us to have a relationship with Him. Yeshua as a genuine spiritual teacher did not teach his disciples to focus on himself. He told them to follow him, and he was showing by his example and teachings that one should develop love for God, whom he was always speaking about. That this relationship was going through him, as it does through a spiritual master or *guru*, is a technicality; the relationship should be with God, even if, at the beginning especially, the relationship with a living spiritual master is very prominent and may be even more with him, God's visible mercy ambassador, than with God Himself. If someone claims to be a follower of Jesus-Christ, then let him follow what he said and did, follow his teachings, the first of which is to love God, whom he called his and our common Father.

"If you're asking whether Jesus expected to be seen as God made flesh, as the living embodiment, the incarnation of God, then the answer to that is absolutely no. Such a thing did not exist in Judaism. In the history of Jewish thought, the notion of a God-man is completely anathema to everything Judaism stands for. The idea

---

[36] Bart D. Ehrman *How Jesus became God*.

that Jesus could have conceived of himself – or that even his followers could have conceived of him – as divine, contradicts everything that has ever been said about Judaism as a religion."[37] Paul claimed that Yeshua was not only the Messiah but also God Himself, which is not at all what the messianic prophecies say. Messiah and God are two totally different things. The prophecies always make distinction between God and the king, His Messiah: *"People will praise God, and they will praise the messiah. People will serve God and they will serve the king, people will bow down to God and they will bow down before the king."* Nowhere in the Bible do you find it announced – contrary to all the *Avatars* of God in the Vedic literature – that God would incarnate in Israel, that the expected Messiah would also be the Supreme Lord. The Jews did not expect a divine Messiah. *"In no place do the Prophets say that he will be anything more than a remarkable leader and teacher...The Jewish Messiah is truly human in origin. He is born of ordinary human parents, and is of flesh and blood like all mortals."*[38]

Introducing monistic ideas

Man, according to the 5th century B.C. Priestly Account of *Genesis*, is *"made in the image and likeness of God."* This is not found in the older, 8th century B.C. Jahvistic version. Indeed, there are two contradictory accounts of Creation found in *Genesis*, the older one after the younger one, differing in many points. The compiler(s) of the final text did not choose one version over the other but simply wrote them in juxtaposition. These contradictions do not stop orthodox Christians to claim the inerrancy of the Bible, whereas early Church Father Origen wrote in *On First Principles*, *"What man of sense will agree with the statement that the 1st, 2nd and 3rd days, in which the evening is named as well as the morning, were without sun, moon and stars? What man is found such an idiot as to suppose that God planted*

---

[37] Reza Aslin, *Zealot*

[38] Rabbi Aryeh Kaplan, *The real Messiah?*

trees in Paradise like a husbandman? I believe every man must hold these things for images under which a hidden sense is concealed." Augustine wrote in the same vein in his *Confessions*, *"There is no way of preserving the 1st chapter of Genesis without impiety and attributing things to God that are unworthy of Him."*

Is it possible for man to become like God, or to become deified, or to become God by grace? Paulinian Christianity precisely holds that Jesus-Christ has made it possible for human beings to be raised to the level of sharing the divine nature. This idea is not characteristically Jewish, although there could be some trace of monism expressed in the Old Testament[39] and Yeshua allegedly quoted it when he was accused of claiming himself son of God;[40] it comes from the mystery religions, where the participant identifies with the deity. Paul clearly seems to have borrowed this idea from them. We have seen that he presented himself as better than Moses, and as good as Yeshua. Or was it his scheme to become godlike as he envisioned Jesus-Christ? Indeed, if you think that your spiritual guide has become God, you will naturally think that it is the ultimate goal. Or maybe it is the other way around: Maybe Paul was a monist who wanted to become one with God, which is the goal of the monists, and he projected that monistic idea on Yeshua. And since his brand of Christianity became the official one, he influenced the subsequent followers of that tradition with his monistic ideas. Indeed, the 2nd century AD Irenaeus had a famous phrase, *"If the Word has been made man, it is so that men may be made gods."*[41] It was repeated almost verbatim by Athanasius in the fourth century," *For He was made man that we might be made God."* Maximus the Confessor had deification as the central idea of his spirituality. Simeon the New Theologian wrote, *"He who is God by nature converses with those whom he has made gods by grace, as a friend converses with his friends, face to face."* Aquinas

---

[39] *Psalm 82:6*

[40] *John 10:34-35*

[41] *Adversus Haereticii V, Preface.*

expresses the same idea of deification, *"The only-begotten Son of God, wanting to make us sharers in his divinity, assumed our nature, so that he, made man, might make men gods."*[42]

Under Paul's influence and due to the paucity of knowledge about the person of God in Christianity, especially about His form, Greek and Russian Orthodox monks do not meditate on God's beautiful form in their practice of Hesychasm – a mystic tradition of contemplative prayer in the Eastern Orthodox Church – but on the "divine light" emanating from Him. They refer sometimes to it as the "uncreated divine light" or "Tabor light", in reference to gospel descriptions of a light emitted by Jesus-Christ during his alleged Transfiguration on Mount Tabor[43] or in Paul's so-called vision. For them, the quintessential purpose and goal of the Christian life is to attain *theosis* or 'deification', understood as "likeness to" or "union with" God, which is obtained by engaging in contemplative prayer. They define God's essence, being, nature and substance (*ousia*) as being beyond all states of consciousness and unconsciousness, existence and non-existence, something and nothing, being and non-being – quite like the impersonal *Brahman* of the Indian *Advaita Vedanta* school of the 8th century monist monk Shankaracharya, which describes it as *neti neti* (nor this nor that). Therefore, they conceive that God in essence is superior to all forms of ontology or being. God's hyper-being is uncreated and therefore incomprehensible to created beings.[44]

According to this tradition, the pure of heart, who have freed themselves from the afflictions of the passions through observance of the commandments of God and ascetic practices (*praxis*), achieve contemplation-union with the divine light. Having attained divine union, they experience a vision of the radiance of the Tabor light. This experience is referred to as *theoria*. The consciousness in a state of ecstasy experiences the

---

[42] *Opusc.* 57, 1-4

[43] Matthew 17:1–8, Mark 9:2–8, Luke 9:28–36

[44] Vladimir Lossky, *The Mystical Theology of the Eastern Church* SVS Press, 1997

infinite and limitless God, who they say is beyond being. *"That is to say, the man who beholds the uncreated light sees it because he is united with God. He sees it with his inner eyes, and also with his bodily eyes, which, however, have been altered by God's action. Consequently, theoria is union with God. And this union is knowledge of God. At this time one is granted knowledge of God, which is above human knowledge and above the senses."*[45]

Simeon the New Theologian (949–1022 AD) describes his vision and mystical union with God as uncreated divine light, *"Oh, what intoxication of light! Oh, what movements of fire! Oh, what swirling of the flame in me, miserable one that I am, coming from You and Your glory!"* (*Hymn* 25) Simeon repeatedly describes the experience of divine light in his writings, as both an inward and outward mystical experience. These experiences came to him during inward prayer and contemplation, and were associated with a feeling of indescribable joy, as well as the intellectual understanding that the light was a vision of God. In his writings, he spoke directly to God about the experience variously as, *"The pure light of your face...You deigned to reveal Your face to me like a formless sun."* He wrote about that divine light, *"It shines on us without evening, without change, without alteration, without form...We bear witness that 'God is light', and those to whom it has been granted to see Him have all beheld Him as light. Those who have seen Him have received Him as light...Those who have not seen His light have not seen Him, for He is the light..."*[46] Although the Christian tradition is officially a path to a personal God, this clearly refers to a vision not of God's personal aspect, but of the undifferentiated, impersonal, luminous *Brahman*, or *brahmajyoti*, of which He is the source.[47]

---

[45] Metropolitan Hierotheos Vlachos, *The Knowledge of God according to St. Gregory Palamas*, Orthodox Psychotherapy Section, published by Birth of Theotokos Monastery, Greece 2005.

[46] *Discourse* XXVIII

[47] *Bhagavad gita* 14.27)

Chapter two

How reliable are the four Gospels?

Many writers deny that Yeshua ever existed historically. They say that he is *"a composite likeness of 20 different persons merged in one"*[48], and that the literature about him was from the beginning not biographical but speculative, that *"it does not depict a real person but a mythological character based upon older myths and heroes."*[49] This controversy has apparently existed from very early on in the history of the Church. The Gnostics were denying that Yeshua, the Christ, had ever been a human being and saw the Gospel as an allegory. The Church fathers had to regularly defend Yeshua's very existence against many philosophers who saw it as a preposterous fabrication with no evidence of it having taken place in history. Christian apologists claim that there are about ten non-Christian sources attesting of Yeshua's existence within 150 years of his life, and ask how could they collectively write a storyline congruent with the Christian authors' stories of the New Testament if he had not existed?[50] However, most of those are contested by many scholars, including Christians, as later forgeries. For instance, in the writings of Flavius Josephus (37-95CE), the renowned Jewish historian, two brief passages appear mentioning Yeshua in *Antiquities of the Jews*. However, as they are stylistically and linguistically very

---

[48] Gerald Massey, *The Historical Jesus and the Mythical Christ*, Health Research, USA 1985

[49] Acharya S. *The Christ Conspiracy*, Adventures unlimited, USA 1999

[50] Norman L. Geisner& Frank Turek, *I don't have enough faith to be an atheist* Crossway books 2004

distinct from the rest of Josephus's work and its context, these are accepted by all non-fundamentalist scholars as later interpolations; or as passages containing later interpolations. People usually think that the early Christian tradition was expressed only in Greek and Latin, but it was translated also in Coptic, Armenian and especially Syriac, a sister language to the Aramaic spoken by Jesus and his people. It was the 3rd international language of the early Church in the 3rd and 4th centuries.

The Syriac translation of the first passage by Josephus goes like this: *"At this time there was a wise man who was called Jesus. His conduct was good and he was known to be virtuous. And many people from among the Jews and the other nations became his disciples. Pilate condemned him to be crucified and to die. But those who had become his disciples did not abandon his discipleship. They reported that he had appeared to them three days after his crucifixion, and that he was alive; accordingly, he was perhaps the Messiah, concerning whom the prophets have recounted wonders"* (*Antiquities* 18.3.3). The Greek translation is as follows: *"Now there was about this time Jesus, a wise man, if it be lawful to call him a man; for he was a doer of wonderful works, a teacher of such men as receive the truth with pleasure. He drew over to him both many of the Jews and many of the Gentiles. He was the Christ. And when Pilate, at the suggestion of the principal men amongst us, had condemned him to the cross, those that loved him at the first did not forsake him; for he appeared to them alive again the third day; as the divine prophets had foretold these and ten thousand other wonderful things concerning him. And the tribe of Christians, so named from him, are not extinct at this day."* When one compares the versions, the obvious embellishment in the latter is striking. The second passage reads as such: *"Festus was now dead [in 62AD], and Albinus was but upon the road; so he [Ananus, the High Priest], assembled the Sanhedrin of judges, and brought before them the brother of Jesus, who was called Christ, whose name was James, and some of his companions; and when he had formed an accusation against them as breakers of the law, he delivered them to be stoned: but as for those who seemed the most equitable of the citizens, and such as were the most uneasy at the breach of the laws, they disliked what was done; they also sent to the king [Agrippa], desiring him to send to Ananus that he should act so no more, for that what he had already done was not to be justified; nay, some of them went also to meet Albinus, as he was upon his journey from Alexandria, and informed him that it was not lawful for Ananus to assemble a sanhedrim without his consent"* (*Antiquities* 20.9). According to the above passage, James, the brother of Yeshua, "who was called Christ", and some others, were killed at the instigation of the High Priest, Ananus, but it created such a tumultuous reaction of the leading Pharisees that they protested. The story goes on saying that the Pharisees had this High Priest deposed by King Agrippa, who replaced him by "Jesus, the son of Damneus." Many scholars have concluded that the James and the first Jesus mentioned here are James and his brother Yeshua (Jesus-Christ). But there is no reference to the death of James, Yeshua's brother, in *Acts*, and both Hegisippus (c110-c180AD) and Clement of Alexandria (c 150-c 215) say he died alone by the hands of an angry mob of priests, thrown from the pinnacle of the temple for having refused to publicly deny his brother, then stoned and clubbed to death. So this passage does not seem to refer to Yeshua nor to his brother James, but to another James and his brother "Jesus, son of Damneus" who was appointed as High Priest after his brother had been killed unjustly by the High Priest Ananus. And the words "who was called Christ" was a later interpolation by a zealous Christian.

Not a single writer before the 4th century makes a single reference to Josephus' wondrous words. The third century

Church Father Origen, for example, spent half his life and a quarter of a million words contending against the Platonist philosopher Celsus who objected to the authenticity of Christian beliefs. Origen drew on all sorts of proofs and witnesses to his arguments in his fierce defense of Christianity. He quotes from Josephus extensively. Yet even he makes no reference to these "golden paragraphs" from Josephus, which would have been the ultimate rebuttal. Origen did not quote these passages from Josephus because they had not yet been written! It is another forgery added to his work at the beginning of the 4th century, during emperor Constantine's reign, probably by Eusebius (c260-c339) according to many scholars. However, absence of irrefutable evidence of Yeshua's life is not synonymous with nonexistence...

So much has been written about the dating and authorship of these writings. [Do we have any of the original documents of the New Testament? No, none of those original writings have survived, or if some have they have not been discovered; but no one expected the discovery of the Dead Sea Scrolls. Are there early copies of the original documents written down in the first century? Yes, almost 15,000 hand-written copies in various languages (9000 in Greek, the rest in Syriac, Coptic, Latin, Arabic). The earliest undisputed one is a segment of John dated by scholars between 117-138CE, found in Egypt. There are 9 earlier disputed fragments dating from 50 to 70 CE found with the Dead Sea Scrolls. The oldest surviving copies of complete New Testament books are from about 200CE and the earliest copy of the whole New Testament is the Codex Vaticanus dated 325CE. But the early Church Fathers of the 2nd and 3rd centuries (like Justin Martyr, Irenaeus, Clement of Alexandria, Origen and Tertullian) quoted the New Testament so much that it could be reconstructed just from their quotations, except about 10 verses. Are the copies available accurate? There are many variants in the manuscripts, mostly in spelling and punctuation; out of 150 000 variants, only 400 change the meaning of the passage, 50 are of real significance, but not one affects an article of the Christian faith. Is the New Testament historically reliable? Yes, it passes the tests historians often use to determine the credibility of historical documents. Some skeptics argue that there are not enough early testimonies and that the available ones are not early enough. To this it can be replied first that most people were illiterate at that time and were living in an oral culture; second, that the followers of Jesus were expecting to see him come back during their own lifetime as he had stated, so they saw no immediate need to write anything and only thought wise to do so when they became old and he had not come back yet.][51]

Actually, the point in question is not if we have early copies of original documents or not. We do, and a good amount; the point is: do they speak the truth? From my personal studies of Christian theology and history, and from reading countless books written by scholars on the subject of Jesus-Christ, I have gathered a particular picture: As far as the New Testament is concerned, most people believe that the authors of the gospels were Yeshua's direct disciples since their names are used. In reality, his disciples were mostly lower-class, illiterate peasants and fishermen who spoke Aramean, his own language. Neither they nor anyone who directly witnessed his mission wrote down anything. They transmitted orally what they remembered about his life. Accounts about him and his teachings were written well after the events allegedly occurred. When someone finally started to document his life, it was at least 40 years after he died. Meanwhile, Paul, if he is at all the author of the letters attributed to him, was apparently the only person documenting anything about Yeshua. His epistles speak in strictly metaphysical terms about "the Christ". He says actually very little about a human being

---

[51] *I don't have enough faith to be an atheist.*

named Yeshua who allegedly lived from about 4 BC to about 35 AD. Where did he learn what he wrote about him? He had hardly any contacts with his disciples. According to *Acts* but not confirmed by Paul, three years after his conversion he met James and Peter for two weeks, then again after eleven years, plus a meeting with Peter in Antioch where they quarreled. He claimed direct revelation, but he knew hardly anything about Yeshua. He did not seem to know about the various Christian dogmas such as the virgin birth, nor about the miracles such as the feeding of five thousand people, the turning water into wine in Cana, the raising of Lazarus, nor about the sermon on the mount or the many parables that Yeshua is said to have spoken.

Those who wrote the gospels were not historians as we define the term today, neither were they eyewitnesses to Yeshua's ministry. Almost all of these eyewitnesses were dead by the time of the gospel writings, either of natural causes or as a result of the Jewish-Roman war that began in AD 66. The gospels were written by people who did not know Yeshua, who did not live in the same country and who did not speak the same language. They were apparently highly educated Greek-speaking Christians writing in Koine Greek. They made Yeshua dispense their own views. The time gap between the events and the first written documentation was long enough for a gradual process of myth-making and legendary embellishments of hagiography somewhat covering the historical accounts. It continued on for decades as can be seen in the more embellished writings of *Matthew, Luke,* and mostly *John*. Modern scholars have concluded that the Canonical Gospels went through various stages in their formation: First, there was what Jeffrey Bütz, author of *The Brother of Jesus*, calls, "*the elusive holy grail of historical Jesus stories: the actual historical events that gave rise to both the oral tradition and the latter written accounts.*" Then the first stage was a multiform oral tradition, which included various stories about Yeshua such as healing the sick, or debating with opponents, as well as parables and teachings. In the second stage, the oral traditions began to be written down in Aramaic or Hebrew as collections of miracles and sayings, while the oral traditions continued to circulate. In the third stage, the written collections and oral traditions were combined into what might be called "proto-gospels" – hence the author of *Luke*'s reference to the existence of many earlier narratives about Yeshua. In the fourth stage, the various compilers of the four Gospels drew on these proto-gospels, collections, and still-circulating oral traditions to produce the gospels attributed to the direct apostles Matthew, Mark, Luke and John. The first three are known as the Synoptic Gospels because they have such a high degree of interdependence. Modern scholars generally agree that *Mark* was the first of the gospels to be written. The author seems to have woven together small collections and individual traditions into a more or less coherent if not historic presentation. It is generally thought that the authors of *Matthew* and *Luke* used as sources *Mark* and other collections of sayings. These two together account for the bulk of each of *Matthew* and *Luke*, with the remainder made up of smaller amounts of source material unique to each, which may have been a mix of written and oral material. Most scholars believe that the author of *John* used oral and written sources different from those available to the Synoptic authors – a "signs" source, a "revelatory discourse" source, and others – although there are indications that a later editor of this gospel may have used *Mark* and *Luke*. My understanding is that after they were written, they were further edited by many hands over time and many forgeries took place, some early some much later. For instance, the episode of the adulterous woman with the famous, "*Let he who has not sinned cast the first stone*" is an 8th century forgery! It is absent from all the earlier manuscripts.

When Jerusalem was destroyed by the Romans in 70 AD, the band of Jewish followers of Yeshua or Nazarenes were decimated. There is an ancient legend of them being warned beforehand of the impending disaster by an oracle and of them fleeing to Pella in Transjordania. The Ebionites say that they come from that group which escaped the slaughter. So, except those and a few who are said to have escaped to Antioch, Caesarea and Alexandria, practically the only people somewhat following Yeshua were the new Roman converts and other Gentiles who were all Paul's followers. This eliminated the opposition to his ideas, which then became the template for his new religion, Christianity. The New Testament books were reworked by his followers after the destruction of Jerusalem. They were fashioned to support this new message, including statements added to make it appear that Jesus-Christ saw himself in the role as envisioned by Paul.[52]Consequently, some of the gospels are told in a manner consistent with Paul's theology, as previously mentioned.[53]

The big controversial debate about whether Yeshua existed, or whether the basic storyline of his life is genuine or not is not the point. He existed and that basic storyline, although incoherent at times, is authentic. The real issue is what was made out of it by Paul as well as by his early and later followers. The crux of the matter is that Paul has interpreted apparently authentic facts by giving them an altogether different meaning.

The point is that the gospels have been written or edited quite early on. The Christian apologists who wrote *I don't have enough faith to be an atheist* [54]make a good job in building their case. One of the arguments which they present, though, as a proof of authenticity of what the evangelists wrote is the fact that the texts contain material which is embarrassing to

---

[52] For instance: *"Anyone who has seen me has seen the father."* (John 14.9)

[53] For instance, to back up Paul's claim of Jesus-Christ as God's only son: *"A voice from heaven said, 'You are my own dear Son, and I am pleased with you.' (MK.1.11),* and *"Then a voice from heaven said, 'This is my own dear Son, and I am pleased with him.'"* (Mt 3.17) and *"And God so loved the world that He sent His only son."* (John 3.16), *"I and the father are one."* (John 10.30)

[54] Norman L. Geisner and Frank Turek

them. However, according to most scholars, that material has been specifically added by Pauline editors of the gospels for the very specific purpose of putting some specific people down. That is how they "got rid" of the direct disciples, especially the "competition" to Paul's status as a leader, so it is not a proof of authenticity at all. The author of *Mark*, who is apparently a Pauline, consistently denigrates those direct disciples, portraying them as stupid ignorant people who are also unable to understand his message, whereas Paul is depicted as the rare genius who alone understood it. He is writing polemically against the leadership of the young Jewish Yeshua movement based in Jerusalem, especially its pillars, Peter and James, who opposed Paul's concoctions and the way he preached to the Gentiles. He makes Yeshua call Peter "Satan". Did Yeshua really do so? He may also have invented Peter's so-called triple denial which the other gospel writers copied or confirmed. He also intentionally and systematically presents with clear animosity Yeshua's family as being unappreciative and even opposed to him and not believing in him nor understanding him – this is a specific polemic against James. He also puts down their successors. He seems to resent their authority and hegemony.

Matthew does not do so. He is apparently a Jewish follower of Yeshua and rebukes Paul's idea of faith versus works and his rejection of the Torah. He is quite bitter about the leaders of the Judaism of his time, the Pharisees, from whom he was apparently recently estranged, but, strangely enough, he seems to retrospectively put both words of praise and strong words of condemnation against them in Yeshua's mouth, literally a blanket demonization of all of them. He seems to have had an axe to grind with them as it reeks of a personal feud, but he projects it back in time on Jesus. According to Papias of Hierapolis he "compiled the oracles in a Hebrew dialect." Papias tried to select around 110 AD some writings to create an official canon, but he was strongly opposed by different communities. To accomplish the same task and select the four "official" gospels among so many writings, around the end of the 2nd century Irenaeus had to threaten the same communities with sanctions if they did not comply and accept his selection.

Luke does not claim to be a direct disciple but a Gentile convert writing by relying on earlier sources.[55] He is also a Pauline, but he whitewashes the history in his liberalism and desire that the church re-unites and the missions reconcile and he falsifies history for that purpose. He writes in *Acts* that Peter was desperate after the crucifixion and went back to his previous life as a fisherman; then Jesus appeared to him and, ashamed, he took up again he preaching work. Peter allegedly had such great healing powers that simply by his handkerchief or his shadow he would cure people; he performed many miracles to propagate the new faith. He is presented as a conciliator between Paul and James. *Acts* speak about a Simon the Magus who was a rival of Peter. Some apocryphal Gospels say that this Simon is no other than Paul...

The author of *John*, the ultra-Pauline, whose Gospel is laden with Gnostic elements as are Paul's Epistles, writes like the author of *Mark*, as if only Paul had understood Yeshua's real nature, message and intentions. He presents the orthodox teachings of the original followers of Yeshua as being heretical and Paul's heresy and travesty of these teachings as being orthodox, as mentioned earlier! What is presented by Luke as two branches of the same mission were never so. They were two separate groups from the start. One was James and the Nazarenes, continuing to follow Jesus' practices, Judaism, and then Paul who started his own movement, Christianity, a new religion incompatible with Judaism because of his ideas which became competitive and antagonistic. The Jews have been pointed at for centuries by the Christians as guilty of deicide, as if God could be killed!? If God can be killed, then He is not God. God is eternal, He does not have a material body subjected to time and death. The Christians do not seem to have a proper knowledge and understanding of God's nature

---

[55] Luke 1:1-3

at all.

An impressive number of German Protestant theologians and philosophers have undertaken a thorough historical exegesis of the Gospels, beginning in the 18th century, and written about Yeshua from different points of view, which are analyzed in the work of the famous Nobel prize winner doctor Albert Schweitzer, *The Search for the historical Jesus*. To give an idea of the very great variety of speculative opinions of these scholars on the subject, I am now presenting their ideas on the basis of that amazingly detailed and complete work. He himself wrote, *"The first three Gospels are written from the Jewish point of view and the fourth from the Greek point of view. The author may have received some material coming from Apostle John, but he has given to the text the Gnosticizing dialectical form of Alexandrian theology."*[56]

Johann Herder, grasping their incompatibility, was the first to recognize in 1796 that all attempts to harmonize the Synoptic Gospels with *John* were unavailing, and that the life of Yeshua/Jesus could be construed either to the former either to the latter but not on both at the same time. He thought that *John* is not a primitive historical source and gives free play to Greek ideas: *"His Gospel is determined much more by its writer's own theological views than by historical concerns and it cannot be therefore regarded as a good source for the life of Jesus. It is a theological rather than a historical document."*

August F. Gfrörer wrote in 1830 that he did not agree with the other historians about the priority of *Mark* and the rejection of *John* as a reliable source for the history of Yeshua's life. He explained that, *"The tradition about Jesus had been passed orally for about two generations and had absorbed much material that was legendary. Luke was the first who checked that process and undertook to separate what was genuine from what was not, keeping closely to his sources and adding nothing of his own, in contrast with the author of Matthew who wrote at a later date and invented matter of his own, insisting to carry*

---

[56] *The Quest for the Historical Jesus*

over the Old Testament into the New. Both Gospels, however, were written long after the destruction of the temple and capital city of Israel, since they do not draw their material from the Jerusalem tradition but from the Christian legends which had grown up around the Sea of Tiberias. They thus mistakenly transferred the scene of Jesus' ministry to Galilea, creating doubts in many Christians even down into the 2nd century about the truth of these two Gospels. The author of Mark is the earliest witness to these doubts of the primitive Christian community. He desired to reconcile the inconsistencies found in his predecessors' works and produce a Gospel composed of materials of which the authenticity could be maintained even against the doubters. He adapted his Gospel to the needs of the Church by leaving out everything that was open to objection in Matthew and Luke. His Gospel was probably produced between 110 and 120. It proves that there was legendary material in the two earlier Gospels."

Christian H. Weisse asked in 1838 how is it possible to explain and make intelligible that

"*John – a man who was a beloved immediate disciple of Jesus, admitted more intimately than any other into the master's confidence, a man who was chosen along with James and Peter as an apostle to the Jews and not to the Gentiles – displays in his thought and speech, in fact in his whole mental attitude, a thoroughly Hellenistic stamp? And how did he come to clothe his master in this foreign garb of Hellenistic speculation and to attribute to him this alien manner of speech? John read by itself would give a completely false conception of the relation of Jesus to the people. The reader would form the impression that the attitude of the people towards Jesus was hostile from the very first, and that it was only in isolated occasions, for a brief moment, that Jesus by his miraculous acts inspired the people with astonishment rather than admiration; that, surrounded by a little company of his disciples, he contrived for a time to defy the enmity of the multitude, and that, having repeatedly provoked it by intemperate invective, he finally succumbed to it. One would never guess from that gospel that Jesus, until his* *departure from Galilea, had experienced almost unbroken success. It is a fixed idea, one may say, with the author of this Gospel, who had heard that Jesus had fallen a victim in Jerusalem to the hatred of the Jewish rulers, that he must represent him as engaged, from his first appearance onward, in an unceasing struggle with 'the Jews', <u>whereas we know</u> that the mass of people, even to the last, in Jerusalem itself, were on the side of Jesus; so much so, indeed, that his enemies were only able to get Him into their power by means of a secret betrayal."*

Indeed, the other gospels state that Yeshua's enemies wanted to arrest him but were afraid of the reaction of the crowd who considered him a prophet, so they did it during the night, and crucified him in the late morning. Weisse writes here "<u>whereas we know</u>" which means he accepts the version of the Synoptic Gospels; but who is to say that he is right in doing so? Maybe it is the author of *John* who is right and he did not mind writing something very different than the earlier Gospels because he knew better. Who can tell? Anyway, the Synoptic gospels and *John* are irreconcilable historically-wise. For instance, the former say that Yeshua went only once to Jerusalem for the Passover festival and was crucified at that occasion. That would make his preaching last barely one year. In *John*, however, we see Yeshua journeying four times to Jerusalem, attending three Passover festivals, which makes his ministry last at least three years. So one has indeed to choose between the former and the latter.

Bruno Bauer wrote in 1840 a skeptical life of Yeshua. The almost unanimous criticism by the previous German historians of *John* as unreliable historically-wise opened the possibility that a gospel may have had a purely literary origin. So, one could deduct that *Mark* – which Bauer thought to be the first written Gospel – also might be of a pure literary origin. In that case, *Matthew* and *Luke* could be purely literary expansions of *Mark*, and like him, purely artistic literary inventions. Bauer thought that, "*The birth stories could not differ so much from each other if they had been derived from tradition, so they are therefore not literary versions of a tradition but possibly literary inventions. And if one applies the same principle to the material additional to Mark found in Matthew and Luke, a similar result appears. So our knowledge of the Gospel history doesn't rest upon any basis of tradition but only upon three literary works. Two of these are not independent, being merely expansions of the first; the third, Matthew, is also dependent upon the second. Consequently, there is no tradition of the Gospel history but only a single literary source."*

When these ideas began to dawn upon Bauer and he began his investigation, he still assumed that what the original Evangelist really did was to portray the life of Yeshua in accordance with the Messianic view of him, just as the fourth Evangelist portrayed it in accordance with the presupposition that he was the revealer of the Logos. It was only later in the course of his investigations that Bauer's opinion became more and more radical. He apostrophized the theologians, reproaching them with not daring, owing to their apologetic prejudices, to see things as they really are, and with declining to face the ultimate results of criticism from fear that the tradition might suffer more loss of historic value than religion could bear. He became obsessed with a fixed idea: "*What if the whole thing should turn out to be nothing but a literary invention – not only the events and discourses but even Jesus himself, the personality who is assumed as the starting point of the whole movement? What if the Gospel history were only a late imaginary embodiment of a set of exalted ideas and these were the only historical reality from first to last?*" His detailed analysis of all the inconsistencies found in the Gospels made him unfortunately conclude that the whole thing was a purely literary creation. He hated the theologians and the web of lie and deceit of their pseudo-science, and also Christianity, which was for him a religion which ought to have led on to the true religion but had usurped its place.

Ludwig Noack in 1876 wrote that, "*The inconsistency in John is not due to a single author but is the result of a long process of redaction in which various divergent tendencies have been at work. But as it is not the logical terminus of the process of alteration, the only alternative is to place it at the beginning. If we cancel from John all Jewish doctrines and miracles, we arrive at the primitive writing composed in 60 by none other than Judas."* So Noack deems Judas to be the mysterious 'beloved disciple' mentioned in John. *"This primitive Gospel aims only at giving a section of Jesus' history, a representation of his attitude of mind and spirit."* The French writer Ernest Renan produced in 1863 the first Life of Yeshua/Jesus for the Catholic world, which had scarcely been touched by the two and a half generations of critical study devoted to the subject by the German Protestant exegetes. For him, the discourses in *John* are not authentic. The historical Yeshua cannot have spoken thus. But he thought that, *"Although all the Gospels are legendary biographies, John remains the best biographer."* In 1882, Gustav Wolkmar opined that, *"The sole source for the life of Jesus was Mark, probably written in 73, five years after the Johannine apocalypse. Matthew and Luke belong to the second century and can only be used by way of supplement, Matthew being a later combination of Mark and Luke. It is a revision of the Gospel tradition in the spirit of that primitive Christianity which was still opposing the tendency of Paul to make light of the Law."*[57]

An "evolution" in the gospels

The gospels are not historically accurate accounts but basically faith documents written to convince and convert new people to the new faith. Retrospective prophecies were employed in them. We have direct evidence that many errors were made in the copying process and that some stories were deliberately added to the orally transmitted Aramaic and Hebrew older material; plus, there were many errors and adaptations made while translating from Greek to other

---

[57] *The Quest for the Historical Jesus*

languages. Remember that the Christian canon was not settled until the middle of the fourth century CE. We do not have even the originals of what the authors of the gospels wrote. According to many scholars and historians, the earliest gospels available are copies of copies of copies[58] of texts written many decades after Yeshua. *"The early Christians were not averse to adding to scripture tales and stories of questionable authenticity. In effect, it means that they had no problem making things up to embellish the accounts. The forged ending portion of Mark contains demonstrably false statements."*[59] The stories told in the gospels tend to become more impressive as each new gospel was written. The writers of the gospels or subsequent editors made revisions to boost the image of Yeshua and to make it appear that he viewed his crucifixion as an expected and necessary part of his earthy mission. In *Mark*, and to a lesser extent, in the later gospels of *Matthew* and *Luke*, Yeshua talks very little about himself and is more focused on his Father and preparing the way for the coming "Kingdom of God". He makes no inferences as to having a divine status. But in *John*, literally everything changes in Yeshua's doctrinal approach. He is principally focused on himself, who he is, and where he came from. *"It's difficult to know how much of what's written in the Gospels is an insight*

---

[58] *"What are extant are hand written copies of copies of copies in the original Greek, with 94 per cent dating from the 9th century... Our earliest copies of Paul's writings come about 150 years after he wrote them. Mistakes and intentional alterations in the copying process resulted in thousands of variations in these texts until the invention of the printing press in the 15th century...There were some deliberate omissions, insertions and mistranslations in the New Testament... The early New Testament was a fluid entity for many decades and determining what was really the Word of God was controversial. Ultimately, men who did not personally know the authors of the scriptures made the decisions..."* http://www.religioustolerance.org/symes02.htm

[59] http://www.biblicalarchaeology.org/daily/biblical-topics/new-testament/the-strange-ending-of-the-gospel-of-mark-and-why-it-makes-all-the-difference/

into how Jesus saw himself and how much is comment of other people as to how they saw Jesus."[60] In *John*, Yeshua touts his status as being divine and equal to God Himself. This is a dramatic departure from the earlier gospels as well as from the traditions of the Jewish faith. Bible scholar Bart Ehrman discusses this point[61]: *"It is inconceivable that if Jesus referred to himself as being divine, this fact would not have been thoroughly documented in the earlier gospels, as this would have been by far the most important message of Jesus's mission. Modern Christianity has fully incorporated the implications of the Gospel of John, precisely defining its doctrine thereby."*

Upon analysis, including of the "non-canon" books of early Christianity, it is actually quite difficult if not impossible to really know what Yeshua actually said. This knowledge has not been transmitted by a line of self-realized souls like the Vedic teachings.[62] What were his own words and what has been attributed to him by the first Christian preachers for converting people or when confronted to opposition and other philosophies? Even Christian scholars admit that the words he allegedly spoke in the New Testament are not *verbatim* quotes, immediately recorded and noted down, but an approximation of the gist of what he taught. That accounts partly for the differences in wording or discrepancies in the Gospels. *John*,

---

[60] Reverend John Bell, leader in the Iona Community and minister of the Church of Scotland 17/09/2009

[61] http://www.npr.org/templates/story/story.php?storyId=124572693

[62] Bhaktivedanta Swami Prabhupada wrote, *"The scriptures of the yavanas, or meat-eaters, are not eternal scriptures. They have been fashioned recently, and sometimes they contradict one another. The scriptures of the yavanas are three: The Old Testament, the New Testament and the Koran. Their compilation has a history; they are not eternal like the Vedic knowledge. Therefore, although they have their arguments and reasoning, they are not very sound and transcendental. As such, modern people advanced in science and philosophy deem these scriptures unacceptable."*

the last gospel, is full of statements which really seem to be preaching arguments disguised as Yeshua's words. For instance, the Samaritan woman saying, *"I know that Messiah is coming"* and Yeshua replying, *"I who speak to you am he."* (4:25-26) How reliable are these quotes? Likewise, the words attributed to him, *"I am the way and the light and no one can go to the Father but through me."* They were probably true in his times and in Galilea, as he had a unique holiness, but they cannot be quoted as words he actually said. They cannot either be extended as a permanent exclusive truth valid for all times as the Christians claim, because *erketai*, the Greek word used, indicates the present, not the future! This is not helping the Christian cause, especially nowadays, as they smack so much of exclusivity and fanaticism. *"The historical Jesus did not make history; the remembered Jesus did...The Gospels we have are not stenographic accounts of the things Jesus said and did. They contain stories which had been in circulation for decades – not simply among disciples but also among all sorts of people – before anyone wrote them down. If we understand what psychologists have told us about memory and false memory, and about how we sometimes actually invent stories in our heads about the past; if we understand what sociologists have told us about collective memory and how our social groups affect and mold the ways we preserve our recollections of past events; and if we understand what anthropologists have learned about how oral cultures not just cherish and preserve but also alter, transform, and even invent their traditions, we will have a much clearer sense of what the Gospels are and of how we should understand the stories they tell about the historical Jesus...Jesus has been "remembered" and "misremembered". We know in fact that these stories were changed, because we can compare different accounts of the same words or activities of Jesus and find discrepancies. Yet other accounts are historically implausible, and so appear to have been created in the years of transmission as people recounted what they had heard about the life of their Savior. The early Christians told stories that remembered Jesus' past in light of the community's present.*

These may have been "distorted" memories in the sense that they involved words and deeds that did not actually go back to the historical Jesus. When it comes to Jesus, all we have are memories, written long after the fact by people who were not actually there to observe him, memories of later authors who had heard about Jesus from others. They are memories of memories of memories."[63]

The parables

Many of the discourses attributed to Yeshua in the Gospels seem to be mere bundles of heterogeneous sayings, as they do not advance from one point to another by the logical development of an idea. Thoughts are merely strung together one after the other, as if they were independent parts of a previous text or oral tradition consisting in a list of sayings which have been artificially assembled. In these discourses, the parables are a kind of enigma. The apologists say that they were meant to make Yeshua's teachings clear and accessible to all, whereas in *Mark* Yeshua himself allegedly contradicted that theory when he unambiguously said to his disciples that he was speaking to the mass of people in a way *"that they might hear but not understand*!?" Since the Gnostics claim that Yeshua entrusted to a limited number of his followers a special knowledge, *gnosis*, by which they would be able to achieve emancipation from the evil world of matter, is that a Gnostic interpolation in the Gospel? If not, what was the point of Yeshua to preach exclusively in parables to the crowds then? To mystify them and repel them?! It doesn't make any sense! Was it, as suggested by Bruno Bauer just to exercise the intelligence of his disciples? In that case, wouldn't it have been much better then, as he also suggested, to do so when they were alone with him? But then we are told that they did not even understand a simple parable like that of the

---

[63] Bart D. Ehrman, *Jesus Before the Gospels*

Sower and needed their rabbi to explain it further to them. Is this then a Pauline interpolation, meant like in many places to make the disciples appear completely dumb and present Paul as a genius who understood the master better than them without having ever seen him?

Bernhard Weiss wrote in 1882 that Yeshua used the parabolic form of discourse as a means of separating receptive, predestined hearers from unreceptive hearers. Indeed, Paul also invented the doctrine of predestination, which is found, for instance, in *Romans*: *"For those whom God foreknew, he also predestined to be conformed to the image of His son, in order that he might be the firstborn among many brothers. And those whom He predestined He also called..."* (8:29-30). Or in *Ephesians*, *"God predestined us for adoption as sons through Jesus-Christ, according to the purpose of His will"* (1:5). *"In Christ we have obtained an inheritance, having been predestined according to the purpose of Him who works all things according to the counsel of His will."* (1:11) The Catholics do not accept this doctrine and it was condemned when it appeared in France in the 17th century in Port-royal under the form of Jansenism. But it is upheld by the Protestants, who interpret Paul's words as teaching predestination. A German scholar like A. Schweitzer therefore finds in this doctrine the reason why Jesus only spoke in parabolic language about the Kingdom of God and why he inexplicably suddenly gave up his preaching in Galilea when it was the most successful, and he "reads it" in the Gospel: [*One reason for this limitation is distinctly stated in Mark 4:10-12 ("And when he was alone, those around him with the twelve asked him about the parables and he said to them, 'to you has been given the secret of the Kingdom of God, but for those outside everything is in parables, so that they may indeed see but not perceive, and may indeed hear but not understand, lest they should turn and be forgiven.'"), viz. predestination! Jesus knows that the truth which he offers is exclusively for those who have been definitely chosen, that the general and public announcement of his message could only thwart the plans of God, since the chosen are already winning their salvation from God...It must be publicly presented only in parables, in order that those only who are shown to possess predestination, by having the initial knowledge which enables them to understand the parables, may receive a more advanced knowledge. The predestinarian view goes along with the eschatology. The ethical idea of salvation and the predestinarian limitation of acceptance to the elect are constantly in conflict in the mind of Jesus...The Beatitudes are also really predestinarian in form. Jesus does not intend the sayings as an injunction or exhortation but as a simple statement of fact: in their being poor in spirit, in their meekness, in their love of peace, it is made manifest that they are predestined to the Kingdom...The Kingdom cannot be earned; what happens is that men are called to it...Jesus in these parables uses the formula, 'he that has hears to hear, let him hear' means that there lies concealed a supernatural knowledge concerning the plans of God which only the pre-ordained can detect...Jesus also speaks of the 'least in the Kingdom of God' according as it has been determined in each individual case from all eternity...*]

For Wilhelm Bousset writing in 1892, "*When we find the Evangelist asserting that the aim of the parables was to mystify and conceal, we may conclude that the basis of this theory is the fact that these parables concerning the Kingdom of God remained unintelligible to Jesus' contemporaries.*" A. Schweitzer thought that this statement may have applied only to one particular parable, but was misunderstood to apply to all of them. He wrote, "*There is something quite incomprehensible in the public ministry of Jesus taken as a whole which lasted less than one year and, upon analysis, dwindles to a few weeks of preaching here and there in Galilea and a few days in Jerusalem...Even Jesus' supposed didactic preaching is not really that of a teacher since he limits himself to the parabolic form of teaching and the purpose of his parables is not to reveal but to conceal, according to Mark 4:34!? His teaching appears as a kind of accessory aspect of his vocation. His always speaking in parables and his suddenly taking the inexplicable resolution to give up a successful preaching field both point back to a mysterious presupposition which greatly reduces the importance of his work as a teacher...In the parables about the kingdom, it is not the idea of development but of the apparent absence of causation which occupies the foremost place. The description aims at suggesting the question, how, and by what power incomparably great results can be infallibly produced by an insignificant fact without human aid. A man sowed seed and did not trouble any further about it, knowing that in time it would yield a great harvest. Much of what he sowed was lost, but the little that fell into good ground yielded a bountiful harvest which left no trace of the lost seeds. How did that come about? By what power was that effected? The parables indicate that the sowing – the movement of repentance evoked by John the Baptist whose times Jesus described as being preparatory to the coming of the Kingdom of God in Matt 11:12, and intensified by Jesus' own preaching – had been done and that, just like a man believes in the harvest following seed-sowing without being able to explain it, one could believe with the same absolute confidence that the Kingdom of God must come, wrung from God by the host of penitents. It must follow by the power of God as certainly as seed-sowing is followed by harvest by the same power. Jesus used the formula 'He that has ears to hear, let him hear', thereby signifying that in these parables there lied concealed a supernatural knowledge concerning the plans of God, which only the fore-ordained could detect whereas these sayings remained unintelligible for others."*[64]

A simpler and more pragmatic reason why Yeshua spoke in parables was maybe because his preaching the coming of the Kingdom of God was a direct political challenge to the *status quo*

---

[64] *The Quest for the Historical Jesus*

of the Pax Romana, and he needed to hide his controversial message under allegories. Indeed, when he entered Jerusalem sitting on a donkey as Zechariah had predicted the king of the Jew would, thus claiming the throne, and soon after chased the merchants and money-changers in the temple precincts, the Romans understood. They took his actions as being highly subversive and threatening to their rule, and so they disposed of him quickly, condemning him as the "king of the Jews".

The lost gospels

The sole fact that the Church held absolute control over intellectual property for more than one thousand years, effectively eliminating much of the knowledge and libraries of the ancient Mediterranean – murdering all of its *intelligentsia* who wanted to remain "pagan" – makes the purported copies of ancient writers under their control entirely suspect, not to mention the proclivity of Christian monks to apply their creative license on ancient texts. The New Testament only represents a small part of the ancient literature written about Yeshua. It is grossly incomplete. There was a great variety within primitive Christianity. There were different communities with different beliefs and different texts. Jewish Christians who held to the ongoing validity of the Law only used *Matthew* and/or the *Didache* also called *The teachings of the twelve apostles*. Some who argued that Yeshua was not really the Messiah only accepted *Mark*. The Montanists favored ongoing prophecy; etc. In other words, there were other versions of the Christian faith than the one which became the official one, some apparently not as much Cross-centered. They were all later on declared heretical by the orthodoxy and persecuted. Marcion (c85-c160), the rich son of a bishop of Sinope in Pontus, Asia Minor, was the first Christian to produce in mid-2nd century a collection of books constituting the sacred texts of the faith, that he called the Apostolicon. He considered Paul the only author of authoritative scriptures and included ten of his epistles, along with a form of what is now *Luke*, which he attributed to Paul. He may have been actually the author of some of these letters. Indeed, one can wonder how he came in possession of letters sent to different communities in different countries. However, as he had a low opinion of Christianity's Jewish origins, he purged them of any reference to Judaism and omitted the whole of the Old Testament. It is in opposition to him that the Church Father Irenaeus of Lyons (AD c.130-c.200), Bishop of Lyons, compiled his own canon, which did include a version of the Old Testament. Marcion based his theology on the contents of the letters of Paul whom he considered as the only one who had understood Yeshua. Many Christian theologians have admitted that the God of the Old Testament is not the same deity described by modern Christianity. As Marcion intelligently reasoned, how can the two testaments be describing the same God? His study of the Hebrew scriptures led him to conclude that many of the teachings of Jesus-Christ were incompatible with the actions of Yahweh, who appears as the jealous, tribal war-deity of the Jews in the Hebrew Scriptures. Marcion developed the understanding that the deity described in the Torah is not the same God spoken of by Yeshua, that he has attributes wholly incompatible. His theology rejected Yahweh and affirmed the divine father of Jesus-Christ as the true God. This Gnostic notion of two gods allowed him to reconcile the contradictions between the Old Covenant of Abraham and the Gospel message. According to him, in his *Antitheses*, the god of the Old Testament, whom he called the Demiurge, is a perfect example of an ancient tribal god. Contrastingly, the God that Yeshua professed is an altogether different being.

Why are there four gospels? Church Father Irenaeus of Lyons (c130-c200AD)[65]stated that,
"Since there are four zones in the world and four principal winds, while the Church is scattered and the pillar and ground of the

---

[65] Irenaeus's writings have not been preserved in the original Greek, and Latin translations show evidence of his views having been edited to erase evidence of his heresy. His idea of the Incarnation was that the *Word* (*logos*) was God the Father incarnate in Jesus Christ — a view now considered heretical. He also held that Jesus died as a ransom paid to Satan, a view that might well have come to be regarded as heretical if it had not been almost universal until the eleventh century.

Church is the Gospel, it is fitting that it should have four pillars" (*Against heresies* 3.11.7). Thus, near the end of the 2nd century, many Christians insisted that these four were the Gospels, not more not less. Debate about the canon continued however for centuries. It is only in the second half of the 4th century that bishop Athanasius of Alexandria produced the definitive official list of the twenty-seven books constituting the New Testament and called it the canon. But the debate lasted longer. It is somewhat paradoxical that so much argument was going on about the content of the official gospels if one considers the fact that most people in those days were illiterate (85%)! The Church has only accepted as authentic those texts which fitted its agenda and official version. The four Canonic gospels were not the only ones. There were many more, some of which have surfaced in Egypt, some in 1886 like the *Gospel of Peter*, some in 1890 and some in 1945. These texts are of great historical, religious, and linguistic significance, because they include the second oldest known surviving manuscripts of works later included in the Old Testament. Those writings show vastly different 'history' than what is found in the Bible. This rich unadulterated repository of scrolls, independent and free from "orthodox" Christian handling, provide much evidence that the Old Testament, like the New Testament, went through many changes engineered by human hands. In the light of those lost gospels quoted by early Christians, mainly Gnostics, one could write a quite different history of early Christianity.

For instance, the *Gospel of Peter* presents the Romans as quite sympathetic to Yeshua's cause and states that the latter did not suffer on the cross. This gospel speaks about what happened during the resurrection, *"The stone in front of the tomb rolled before the astonished guards. Two men entered the grave and came out holding a third one; a cross followed them, floating in the air. A voice was heard, 'Have you preached to those who fell asleep?' The cross answered affirmatively with a human voice. The three men then rose in the sky, assuming huge forms touching the clouds.*" Scholars have dated this manuscript to the 8th century, some other fragments to the 5th, but it was quoted by various Christian authors around 150AD. It contains elements from the four other gospels. It was a common practice to attribute a text to an earlier authority. This kind of claim has been spotted by scholars as a characteristic device used by later writers to pretend they are an earlier famous character. If this *Gospel of Peter* is not deemed authentic, then it can be argued that the four others are also not, that they are also pseudepigraphical and have been attributed to the apostles but must have been written by their disciples or grand-disciples. The Christians were persecuted by Nero, who committed suicide four years later. Peter fled Rome under a disguise; he met Yeshua on the road and asked him, "*Quo vadis, domine, where are you going, my Lord?*" Yeshua answered, "*I am going to Rome to be crucified again.*" Then Peter went back to Rome where he later met his end... The *Gospel of Thomas*, of which copies dated between 300 and 400AD have been found, does not contain a biographical narration, simply words of Yeshua that are also found in the canonic Gospels. It has a Gnostic mood. It states that all can become sons of God if they follow Yeshua's example, a statement also found in *John* 1:12.

The *Gospel of Mary Magdalena* stresses the role of *sophia* or wisdom. There was a rivalry between her and Peter, who nonetheless acknowledged, "*We know that the savior loved you more than the other women. Tell us the words of the Savior which you remember – which you know (but) we do not, nor have we heard them.*" He had difficulty accepting her answer and said, "*Did he then speak secretly with a woman, in preference to us, and not openly? Are we to turn back and all listen to her? Did he prefer her to us?*" He is then told by another disciple, "*Surely the Savior knows her very well. That is why he loved her more than us...If the savior has made her fit, who are you to reject her?*" The accusation that Mary Magdalena was a former prostitute possessed by demons that Yeshua exorcised is maybe a calumny on the part of

Peter's followers. According to some tradition, she was one of the heads among the apostles. This gospel is dated to the 5th century but older copies of it dated to 200AD were found in Egypt. It does not speak of a paradise after death but of a journey of the soul, with both angelical and demoniac visions. There were also the *Gospel of the Hebrews*, the *Gospel of Philip*, who speaks of Yeshua as the *"companion of Mary Magdalena, whom he often kissed"*, the *Apocalypses of Peter* and the *Shepherd of Hermias* which were also popular texts in the early centuries. This apocryphal[66]literature reveals that they were two main opposed groups of early Christians: the Gnostics, allegedly backed by Mary Magdalena, who preached a direct relationship with God without the need for a hierarchy and bishops, and stressed the importance of *gnosis*, special sacred spiritual knowledge, a bit like the Vedic *jnana*; and the "Orthodoxy", the followers of Paul's current, more political than religious, concerned with having an official dogma, unity, an ideological basis, a uniform faith; the latter were later controlled by the emperor and willing to keep only the texts adapted to the new beliefs. The independence of the Gnostics rendered the authority of the clergy fragile. In 382, other Gospels were banned and destroyed under the laws of emperor Theodosius. Other currents of thought within Christianity which were still prevalent were deemed heretical and their followers persecuted.

In addition to the copying errors made by scribes, there is evidence that the Church and those associated with the Church undertook a concerted campaign to "improve" scripture for the edification of its growing audience of followers. This behavior is justified directly in the New Testament, where Paul writes in the

---

[66] The Greek word *apokruphon* means secret or hidden. After the official canon was established, all the writings related to Yeshua issued from the first Christian communities, which had not been included in it, gradually became suspicious and known as apocryphal. Some say that they were rejected and hidden or destroyed because they were susceptible to question the dogmas and power of the Church.

3rd Chapter of *Romans*, "*For if the truth of God has more abounded through my lie unto His glory, why yet am I also judged as a sinner?*" This deception was justified as an effective means to draw people into the faith by making it easier for them to accept the "truth" of its claims. While discussing having a doctrinally unsuitable part of the *Gospel of Mark* removed, Bishop Clement of Alexandria wrote, "*Not all true things are to be said to all men.*" Eusebius said that, "*It is permissible for Christians to lie in order to further the Kingdom of God*". He writes in his *Ecclesiastical History*, "*We shall introduce into this history in general only those events which may be useful first to ourselves and afterwards to posterity.*"[67] There are further admissions of outright lying to spread their doctrines by Augustine, Jerome and John Chrysostom amongst others, and continued by later religious authorities like the founder of Protestantism, Martin Luther. Here is a quote from a letter written by him, "*What harm would it do if a man told a good strong lie for the sake of the good and for the Christian church ... such lies would not be against God, He would accept them.*"[68]

The variations found in the Gospels do not seem to jeopardize, however, the cardinal or essential message and fundamentals, as the first forgeries date from the writing of the Gospels themselves or their later edition. Only a small percentage of the variants affect the meaning to some degree, like the Greek words for 'food', *brosimus*, or 'table', *trapeza*, being unscrupulously translated as 'meat' by carnivorous Christians. Of course, we have multiple translations in English and other languages that over time modernized the terminology but also inserted changes in meaning. Some elements of the Bible were edited out in later editions. So there have been many interpretations of the Bible, and changes are made up to now by various branches...

---

[67] Vol. 8, Ch. 2

[68] Cited by his secretary, in a letter in Max Lenz, ed. Briefwechsel Landgraf Phillips des Grossmüthigen von Hessen mit Bucer, vol. I.

The authenticity of Paul's epistles

The epistles of Paul represent more than fifty percent of the New Testament (14 out of 27 texts). Many scholars question whether these epistles, or all of them, were actually written by him. The Dutch Radical Critics, for instance, opine that he wrote none of them. Some say that many are pseudepigraphical and were written much later, around 150CE, by members of various Pauline schools of thought. There is something of a consensus that *Romans*, 1 and 2 *Corinthians, Galatians, Philippians,* 1 *Thessalonians* and *Philemon* were penned by him. However, in the 1896 Oxford Bible edition, the original authors of all but two of the epistles are recorded as being different from Paul. [69]The Catholic Encyclopedia admits that some were forgeries and the genuine ones were later falsified.[70] Indeed, as written by Robert Price in the introduction to his mighty work, *The Amazing Colossal Apostle, "Both the Gospels and the epistles are collections of fragments and pericopae contributed and fabricated by authors and communities of very different theological leanings."*[71]They contradict each other at times, and many are anachronistic. They contain a lot of Gnostic material and were indeed very much appreciated by the Gnostics. As Paul had become, according to Tertullian, the "apostle of the heretics, he had to be "domesticated", so the epistles were later edited and sanitized by orthodox catholicizing interpolations.

---

[69] Tony Bushby, *The Bible Fraud*, The Pacific Blue Group Inc. 2001

[70] Vol.VII, p 645

[71] Signature Books, Salt Lake City, 2012

Chapter three
The Messiah

The Messianic idea goes back to the Davidic kingdom. It was reinforced by Zoroastrian influence during the Babylonian exile. The "prophets" raised it to a higher religious plane, but from the times of the Maccabees, if the people dreamed of a messiah, the ideal of the kingly Messiah was what they believed in, not that of a super-earthly deliverer. Externally, the role of an apocalyptic prophet, in the line of previous Jewish apocalyptic prophets of the Old Testament down to John the Baptist, is what seems to define Yeshua and his ministry. They all predicted the ending of the world. Yeshua may have felt it was his mission in life or he may have received that inspiration from his baptizer John – who may actually have been more his spiritual master than just his baptizer – convinced by him that the Day of Judgement predicted by the prophet Daniel was imminent and the "Kingdom of God" soon to come. Or he may have simply chosen to use those beliefs to preach his message of love of God. Some say he lived within his mind in an eschatological world. Who knows? What was his own self-understanding? It is quite subjective. We have unfortunately no direct information about what was Yeshua's psychology, so we can only make more or less educated guesses and deductions. I am also sharing here the views of German scholars to show the variety of opinions, on the same basis of the work of A. Schweitzer.

Did Yeshua think of himself as the Messiah?

If he did, some say it was at his baptism. John the Baptist spoke of one who would baptize with the Holy Spirit. Had it ever been presented as the work of the Messiah to baptize? Some like Christian Weisse say Yeshua had started before, *"He gradually cast off the mundane Messianic ideas of Judaism during his ministry and developed a spiritual conception of the Messiahship, but he did not allow the people to see that he held himself to be the Messiah until he entered in Jerusalem. It was precisely in order to avoid declaring his Messiahship that he kept away from the capital where the priests and scribes would soon have put this question to him, whereas in Galilea he could teach without being obliged to make an explicit declaration about it.*" Some say it is long after his baptism that he thought himself to be the Messiah... If he did think himself to be such, did he have a conception of himself as a Davidic or political messiah as the Jews supposedly expected? It does not seem so according to the Gospels. He was allegedly called 'Son of David' a few times, but he rejected that role. Was there a gradual development of his consciousness as many have suggested? Did he later develop a spiritual conception of the Messiahship? Did he ever openly made himself known as the Messiah, whether to his disciples or to the public? For August Gfrörer, "*Jesus' Messiahship was not political but spiritual; he had declared himself to be in a certain sense the longed-for Messiah, but in another sense he was not so.*" David Strauss wrote in 1835 that, "*The image of the Messiah was a mask which Jesus himself was obliged to assume, and which legend afterwards substituted for his real features.*"[72]

How did Yeshua's disciples see him?

Another subjective question. Most probably they had different ideas and opinions, and that too at different periods of his ministry. They followed him as their teacher, their *rabbi*. Did they identify him as Daniel's apocalyptic "Son of Man" when he was mentioning that term? Was this term understood by the common people as referring to the Messiah? Did Yeshua himself

---

[72] *The Quest for the Historical Jesus*

use that term with the intention of making himself known as the Messiah? If so, Weisse asked, *"Why did he repeatedly refused Messianic salutations? Or did he use that term, which sums up in itself the whole spiritualization of the Messiahship, with the intention that this mysterious designation would compel his hearers to reflect upon its meaning, a reflection that would lead them on to higher conceptions of his nature and origins?"* Did his disciples understand he meant himself or someone else? Did they see him as the Messiah expected to deliver Israel from the Romans and glorifying her among all nations? It seems so. Maybe they started to see him as such after the incident at Caesarea Philippi, just before travelling up to Jerusalem, when Peter called him as such and Yeshua acknowledged it; or maybe only after his appearances after the crucifixion. One thing is sure: they never saw him as their Savior dying for their sins, what to speak of his being one with God, two speculative beliefs which emerged later from the pens of Paul.

Bruno Bauer asked, *"Who is to assure us that the Gospel history, with its assertion of the Messiahship of Jesus, was already a matter of common knowledge before it was fixed in writing and did not first become known in a literary form? In the latter case, one single man would have created out of general ideas the definite historical tradition in which these ideas are embodied. The only thing which could be set against this literary possibility, as an historical counter-possibility, would be a proof that, at the period when the Gospel history is supposed to take place, a general Messianic expectation really existed among the Jews, so that a man who claimed to be the messiah and was recognized as such, as Mark represents Jesus to have been, would be historically conceivable? This presupposition had hitherto been unanimously accepted by all former German writers of Lives of Jesus. But where did they get their information from, apart from the Gospels? Where is the documentary evidence of the Jewish Messianic doctrine on which that of the Gospels is supposed to be based? Daniel was the last of the prophets. Everything tends to suggest that the mysterious content of his work remained without influence in the subsequent period. If, at the time when the Christian community was forming its view of history and the religious ideas which we find in the Gospels, the Jews had already possessed a doctrine of the Messiah, there would have been already a fixed type of interpretation of the Messianic passages in the Old Testament, and it would have been impossible for the same passages to be interpreted in a totally different way, as referring to Jesus and his work, as we find them interpreted in the New Testament. Did the earliest Evangelist not venture to carry back into the history the idea that Jesus had claimed to be the Messiah, because he was aware that in the time of Jesus no general expectation of the Messiah had prevailed among the Jews?"*

There was the expectation of a messiah, but not a general one; it was only among the secretive sects of the Essenes and Zealots. *"When the disciples in Caesarea Philippi reported the opinions of the people concerning Jesus, they could not mention anyone who held him to be the Messiah. Peter was the first one who did so. But Jesus forbade his disciples to tell the people who he was. Why is the attribution of the Messiahship to Jesus made in this surreptitious and inconsistent way? The dogma of the messiah was not therefore apparently taken over ready-made from Judaism, although it is certainly found in its pre-Christian literature, like the Book of Daniel."* For Bauer, the arising of the idea that the Yeshua of the Gospels was the Messiah was only the imaginative conception of the Church. Everything that is said of the historical Christ, everything that is known about him, that is of the imagination of the Christian community. Timothée Colani in 1864 wrote that, *"The general expectation of the Jews in Jesus' times was focused rather upon the Forerunner than upon the Messiah. Up to the incident in Caesarea Philippi, Jesus had never designated himself as the Messiah, for the expression 'Son of Man' carried no Messianic associations for the multitude. In Mark 12:35-37, Jesus' interpretation of Psalm 110 makes known that the Messiahship has nothing whatsoever to do with the Davidic kingship. It was only with difficulty that he came to resolve to accept the title of Messiah. He knew what a weight of national prejudices and hopes hung upon it. He created the expression 'Son of Man' in order thereby to make known his lowliness."*[73] It is quite ironical that Yeshua is said to have used that expression "Son of Man" again and again (99) to designate himself but he was nonetheless later branded the "Son of God" in blatant contradiction!

According to Friedrich W. Ghillany writing in 1864, *"Jesus held himself to be the Messiah and expected the early coming of the 'Kingdom of God'.* Ghillany claims that, *"The Rabbis distinguished two Messiahs, one of Israel, who was to suffer death at the hands of the Gentiles to make atonement for the sins of the Hebrew nation; and one who would come only after, the one predicted by Daniel, the son of David of Judah, appearing in glory upon the clouds of heaven and establishing the Messianic kingdom."* However, this distinction of the two Messiahs is actually not clear even in the Rabbinical writings. For Ghillany, *"The Messianic expectation, being directed to supernatural events, had no political character. One who knew himself to be the Messiah would expect all things to be brought about by the Divine intervention. He did not seek to found a kingdom among men. He waited with confidence. Jesus went to Jerusalem and tried to rouse the Jews to Messianic enthusiasm in order to compel Jehovah to intervene and come to their aid with his heavenly hosts. From the reaction of Jehovah, it could then be discovered whether the preaching of repentance and baptism would suffice to make atonement for the people before Jehovah or not. If Jehovah did not appear, a deeper atonement was to be made. The confession of faith of the primitive Christian community was the simplest conceivable: Jesus the Messiah had come, not as temporal conqueror but as the Son of Man foretold by*

---

[73] *The Quest for the Historical Jesus*

David. In other respects, they were strict Jews and kept the Law. Only the community of goods and the brotherhood-meal were of an Essene Character. The Christianity of the original community in Jerusalem was thus a mixture of Zealotism and Mysticism, which did not include any wholly new element, and even in its conception of the Messiah had nothing peculiar to itself except the belief that the Son of Man predicted by Daniel had already come in the person of Jesus, that he was now enthroned at the right hand of God and would again appear as the expected Son of Man upon the clouds of heaven according to Daniel's prophecy."

Ghillany proposed to found a new Church combining only what was according to reason in Judaism and Christianity. From Judaism, it was to take the belief in one sole, spiritual perfect God and eliminate the ritual system and the sacrifices; from Christianity, the requirement of brotherly love to all men, eliminating the deification of Yeshua and the teachings of redemption through his blood. Wilhelm Bousset wrote in 1892, "*In contrast with his contemporaries, Jesus had a living idea of God. His faith in the fatherhood of God signified a breach with the transcendent, impersonal, Jewish idea of God. Jesus was a manifestation of the ancient undercurrent of a purer and more spontaneous piety present in post-exilic Judaism. He desired to communicate this personal piety by his personal influence on people. Free from all extravagant Jewish delusions about the future, he was not paralyzed by the conditions which must be fulfilled to make this future present.*" Contrary to Bauer, for him, "*It was among the most certain things in the Gospel that Jesus in his earthly life acknowledged himself as Messiah both to his disciples and to the High Priest and made his entrance in Jerusalem as such. The righteousness he preached is one of the goods of the kingdom of God, so he cannot have thought of the kingdom as wholly transcendental. The reign of God began for him in the present era. In the new social righteousness that he preached, the kingdom of God was already present. He didn't clearly explain it, however, but set it forth in paradoxes and parables.* A. Schweitzer questioned if it is so certain that Jesus made a Messianic entry into Jerusalem and that accordingly he declared himself to the disciples and to the High Priest as Messiah in the present and not in a purely future sense. *"The presence of the kingdom of God was only asserted by Jesus as a kind of paradox. Did Jesus preach and work as Messiah, or was his career, historically regarded, only the career of a prophet with an undercurrent of Messianic consciousness?"*

According to Albert Réville, *"Both Apocalyptic and Messianism are foreign bodies in the teachings of Jesus which have been forced into it by the pressure of contemporary thought. Jesus would have never of his own motion taken up the role of Messiah."* For Gustav Wolkmar, as regards the Messianic expectations of the times, Yeshua could not possibly have come forward with Messianic claims: *"The Messianic Son of Man, whose aim was to found a super-earthly kingdom, only arose in Judaism under the influence of Christian dogma. Jesus' contemporaries knew only the political ideal of the Messianic king. And woe to anyone who conjured up these hopes! The Baptist had done so by his too fervent preaching about repentance and the kingdom soon to come, and he had been promptly put out of the way by the Tetrarch. Had Jesus desired the Messiahship, he could only have claimed it in this political sense. The alternative is to suppose that he did not desire it. It suggests that Jesus set himself up as Messiah, but in another sense than the popular sense. What may be called his Messianic consciousness consisted solely in knowing himself to be the first-born among many brethren, the Son of God after the Spirit and consequently believing himself enabled and impelled to bring about that regeneration of his people, which alone could make it worthy of deliverance. It is in any case clearly evident from Paul, the Apocalypse and Mark – the three documentary witnesses emanating from the circle of the followers of Jesus during the 1st century – that it was only after his crucifixion that Jesus was hailed* *as the Christ or Messiah and never during his earthly life. When Peter called him the Messiah in Caesarea Philippi, it was at the time when his ministry was practically over, and Jesus told him not to make his Messiahship known until after his resurrection (Mark 8:30, 9:9-10), which is a hint that we have to date Jesus's Messiahship from his death, for Mark is no mere naïve chronicler. The historical Jesus therefore founded a community of followers without advancing any claims to the Messiahship. He desired only to be a reformer, the spiritual deliverer of the people of God, to realize upon earth the kingdom of God and to extend the reign of God over all nations."*

Bruno Bauer was of the opinion that the way in which Jesus made known his Messiahship was based on another theory of the original Evangelist. He questioned the assumption that it was only at Caesarea Philippi, in the closing period of his life, that Jesus made himself known as the Messiah, and that, therefore, he was not previously held to be so either by his disciples or by the people. The implied course of events, however, is determined by the author of *Mark's* artistic attempt to present a coherent storyline, not by the chronology he proposes, because as history it seems inconceivable. *"Could there be indeed a more absurd impossibility? Jesus must perform these innumerable astounding miracles because, according to the view which the Gospels represent, he is the Messiah – he must perform them in order to prove himself to be the Messiah – and yet no one recognizes him as the Messiah! Mark thus represents a Jesus who does miracles and who nevertheless does not thereby reveal himself to be the Messiah. He was obliged so to represent him because he was conscious that Jesus was not recognized and acknowledged as Messiah by the people, nor even by his immediate followers in the unhesitating fashion in which those of later times imagined him to have been recognized. Mark's conception and representation of the matter carried back into the past the later development by which there finally arose a Christian community for which Jesus had been made the Messiah. His 'artistic design' is completely marred when Jesus does miracles which must have made him known to very child as the Messiah. We cannot therefore blame the author of Matthew very much if he contradicts the plan found in Mark by making Jesus clearly designate himself as the Messiah at an earlier point and many recognizing him as such. And the fourth Evangelist cannot be said to be destroying any very wonderful work of art when he gives the impression that from the very first anyone who wished could recognize Jesus as the Messiah. The author of Mark does not keep strictly to his own plan and makes Jesus forbid his disciples to make known his Messiahship. How then does the multitude at Jerusalem recognize it so suddenly, after a single miracle they had not even witnessed and which was in no way different from others which he had done before? The incident at Caesarea Philippi is the central fact of the Gospel history, it gives us a fixed point from which to group and evaluate the other statements of the Gospel. At the same time, it introduces a complication into the plan of the life of Jesus, because it necessitates the carrying through of the theory – often in the face of the text – that previously Jesus had never been regarded as the Messiah; and lays upon us the necessity of showing not only how Peter had come to recognize his Messiahship, but also how he subsequently became messiah for the multitude – if indeed he ever became the Messiah for them."*

Bauer also discovered the difficulty involved in the conception of miracle as a proof of the Messiahship of Jesus: How do we know that the Messiah was expected to appear as an earthly wonder-worker? There is nothing to that effect in Jewish writings. And don't the Gospels themselves prove that any one might do miracles without suggesting to a single person that he might be the Messiah? *"Accordingly, the only inference to be drawn from Mark is that miracles were not among the characteristic marks of the Messiah, and that it was only later in the Christian community, which made Jesus the miracle-worker into Jesus the Messiah, that* this connection between miracles and Messiahship was established." Bauer also logically exposed the historical and literary impossibility of Jesus having been hailed by the people as messiah: *"Set aside the two references to the Son of Man in Mark 2:10 and 28, Jesus had never, previous to the incident in Caesarea Philippi, given himself out to be the Messiah or been recognized as such. Why had he made a secret of his Messiahship even to his disciples until that moment? Were the people ever made acquainted with His Messianic claims, and if so, when and how?"*

Wilhem Brandt asserted in 1893 that, *"Little of the real history of Jesus is preserved in the Gospels, which are not purely historical sources but also, and in a very much larger degree, poetic invention. Jesus died and was believed to have risen again: this is the only absolutely certain information that we have regarding his life. Jesus was a Galilean teacher and yet is said to have believed himself to be the Messiah. The duality is a cleavage between his conviction and consciousness on the one hand, and his public attitude on the other. Jesus cannot possibly have come forwards as Messiah during the last few days at Jerusalem. The course of events does not at all suggest a Messianic claim on the part of Jesus, indeed, it contradicts it. On the other side, we have the report of his Messianic entry in which Jesus not only accepted the homage offered to him as Messiah but went out of his way to invite it; and the people must therefore from that point onwards have regarded him as the Messiah. This is a big contradiction in the narrative. The logical inference can rigorously be drawn: Since Jesus did not stand and preach in the temple as Messiah, he cannot have entered Jerusalem as Messiah. Therefore, his allegedly well-known Messianic entry is not historical. He was simply hailed as a wonder-worker, at best a prophet, without any Messianic color which was added later. That is also implied by the manner of his arrest. If Jesus had come forward as a Messianic claimant, he would not simply have been arrested by the civil police; Pilate would have had to suppress a revolt by military force."*

Brandt was convinced that, *"Jesus did not go to Jerusalem to die, but he went there to preach to the Jewish leadership to help him convince the people of the need to repent before the coming of the Day of the Lord. The predictions of the Passion are therefore unhistorical. It was only in the capital that the Messianic consciousness entered into Jesus' thoughts, but not at all a political Messiahship. After the crucifixion, his disciples could not continue to believe in his Messiahship unless something occurred to restore their faith, as he had taken away with him in his death the hopes which they had set upon him, especially as he had not foretold his death, much less his resurrection. They returned to Galilea where they had enthusiastic visions of their master."* J. Meinhold was also of the opinion in 1896 that Jesus did not purpose to be the Messiah of Israel.

Paul Wernle wrote in 1901 that, *"The idea of the Messiah, since there was no appropriate place for it in connection with the kingdom of God or the new Earth, had become obsolete for the Jews themselves. The inadequacy of the Messianic idea for the purposes of Jesus is therefore self-evident. He labored to give a new and higher content to the Messianic title which he had adopted. In the course of his endeavor he discarded the 'Messiah of the Zealots', the non-transcendent Messianic ideal."* A. Schweitzer objected, saying that, *"We don't have any knowledge that such an ideal existed in the times of Jesus; the statements of the Jewish historian Josephus and the conduct of Pilatus at the trial of Jesus confirm the conclusion that in none of the previous uprisings did a claimant of the Messiahship come forward; this should be proof enough that there did not exist at that time a political eschatology alongside of the transcendental."* Paul Wernle is of the opinion that, *"The kingdom of God was not for Jesus a purely eschatological entity, but it always remained a supernatural entity. In and with the titles and expressions borrowed from apocalyptic thought – Messiah, Son of God, Son of Man – which* were all at bottom so inappropriate to Jesus and were from the first a misfortune for the "new religion", early Christianity slipped in again either the old ideas or new ones misunderstood." A. Schweitzer asked how had Wernle discovered in the preaching of Jesus anything that can be called historically a new religion, and what would have become of this new religion apart from its apocalyptic hopes and dogma. For him, without its intense eschatological hope, the Gospel would have perished from the earth, crushed by the weight of historic catastrophes.

For Emil Schurer writing in 1903, *"Jesus' reserve in regard to his Messiahship was his fear of kindling political enthusiasm; it is for the same reason that he repudiated all claim to be the Messiah of David's line (Mark 12:37) The ideas of the Messiah and the kingdom of God underwent a transformation in his use of them. If in his earlier preaching he only announced the kingdom as something future, in his later preaching he emphasized the thought that in its beginnings it was already present."* A. Schweitzer suggested that, *"The complete lack of connection between passages in Mark, with all its self-contradictions is due to the fact that two representations, two conceptions of the ministry of Jesus have been crushed into one: a natural one and a deliberately supernatural one. It is not an historical representation of his life but a supra-historical dogmatic religious view. The inconsistency between the public life of Jesus and His Messianic claim lies in the representation of the Evangelist. Jesus cannot have spoken of his Messianic coming in the way which he reports; his openly revealed Messiahship is a product of Mark's author correcting history according to his own conceptions, in order to give a Messianic form to the earthly life of Jesus, whereas nothing was known of a Messianic claim by Jesus himself during his life upon earth. Since the Messianic secret in Mark is always connected with the resurrection, the date at which the Messianic belief of the disciples arose must be the resurrection, which created a sudden revolution in their conception of him. They found it impossible previously to think of him as Messiah. They guessed him to be a prophet. The Messiah was a supernatural personality who was to appear in the last time and who was not expected upon earth before that. But, how is it that the appearances of Jesus after the resurrection suggested to them that Jesus, their crucified teacher, was the Messiah? Apart from any expectations, how can this conclusion have come to them from the mere fact of the resurrection? The fact of the appearances did not by any means imply it. Their coming to that conclusion implies some kind of Messianic eschatological references on the part of the historical Jesus. In other words, it must be that Jesus had given them some hints about it."*

Indeed, there had been the event called the Transfiguration. A. Schweitzer understood and nicely explained that the author of *Mark*, followed by the author of *Matthew*, had inadvertently reversed the order of the episodes of the Transfiguration and of the revelation of Jesus' Messiahship at Caesarea Philippi. After all, as seen earlier, the author of *Mark* was apparently only piecing together the best he could bits and pieces of various traditions, whether oral or written, reported by Peter, which he may not have thoroughly understood. He may not have had a clear idea of the incoherence of the course of events as he reported them and mostly just handed a tradition; he may not have had either a specific opinion concerning the historical life of Yeshua. *"Paul showed that the earthly life of Jesus was regarded with complete indifference by primitive Christianity. The discourses in Acts too. Primitive theology had an eschatological orientation and was dominated by the expectation of the Parousia. It was simply a theology of the future with no interest in history."* During the Transfiguration, Peter, James and John, which constituted the inner circle of the group, received the secret of the Messiahship of Yeshua, not from himself but allegedly from a voice from heaven. On the way down from the mount, Yeshua told them not to repeat to anyone what they had heard until after the resurrection of the "Son of Man". Then at Caesarea Philippi, when he asked the group who the people thought he was and then who did themselves think he was, Peter betrayed the secret of his' Messiahship. Yeshua showed no trace of joy, but was astonished at Peter's impulsively disregarding his order given during the descent from the mount, and told him that *"flesh and blood have not revealed that to you but the heavenly Father"*. A. Schweitzer wrote that, *"It is probable that Jesus had never intended to reveal the secret of his Messiahship to his disciples, otherwise he would not have hidden it from them when he sent them in mission. It was wrung from him by force by Peter's inopportune statement. What Jesus personally revealed to his disciples was not his Messiahship but the secret of his future sufferings. These predictions of his sufferings, death and resurrection are historically inexplicable since the necessity of his death doesn't arise out of the historical course of events."*

Yeshua is said by many Christians to have identified himself as the "suffering servant" of Isaiah, although it doesn't seem that the Jews, if they expected a messiah, expected him to be someone else than a deliverer of his people from the foreign yoke. But since we are told that they expected one and he was unanimously conceived of as a victorious military figure and never as a suffering servant, Peter understandably objected but Yeshua rebuked him. Why? If that passage which first glorifies Peter as being the first one to acknowledge Yeshua as the Messiah was not later edited to put down Peter and the words put in Yeshua's mouth are accurate, Yeshua possibly rebuked Peter because his understanding, based on what we read in the Gospels, was that a period of very intense tribulation was coming; during it, he himself would have to suffer, and his disciples would be rejected and suffer too – with some passing the test and others failing, some surviving the ordeal and some dying – then he would be vindicated by his heavenly father, be transported to heaven and quickly come back at the peak of that tribulation and triumph over the enemy; then he would preside over the final judgment, assisted by the angels, and the "Kingdom of God" would be established for one thousand years, with Israel being glorious over all the nations.

I am writing that it was possibly Yeshua's understanding because we do not know. Did he think himself to be the Messiah? And if so, did he allow the people to see that he thought himself to be the Messiah before entering Jerusalem in triumph, if that event ever really happened? He made no attempt to lay claim to this title. He was, however, officially crucified by the Romans on the accusation of claim to be the Messianic king of the Jews. A. Schweitzer suggested that, *"Jesus maybe saw himself fulfilling the role of Messiah in the future; his death was the deed by which he thought to win the Messiahship proper to the 'Son of Man'. We are without any indication of a thread of connection in the actions and discourses of Jesus because the sources give no hint of the character of his self-consciousness...All what we know of the development of Jesus and of his Messianic self-consciousness has been arrived at by a series of working hypotheses...It may be maintained by the aid of arguments drawn from the sources that his self-consciousness underwent a development during the course of his ministry; it may, with equally good grounds, be denied. Each view equally involves a violent treatment of the text. Furthermore, the sources exhibit, each within itself, a striking contradiction. They assert that Jesus felt himself to be the Messiah; and yet from their presentation of his life it doesn't appear that he ever publicly claimed to be so. They attribute to him an attitude which has absolutely no connection with the consciousness which they assumed that he possessed...We have two hypotheses: either he felt himself to be the Messiah, as the sources assert, or he did not feel himself to be so, as his conduct implies... Does the difficulty of explaining the historical personality lie in the history itself, or only in the way in which it is represented in the sources? ...The self-consciousness of Jesus cannot be illustrated or explained. All that can be explained is the eschatological view in which the man who possessed that self-consciousness saw reflected in advance the coming events, both those of a general character and those which especially related to himself."*

A. Schweitzer, who was also a Christian mystic, developed further his opinion that Yeshua's resolve to suffer and die is dogmatic and although looking unhistorical is actually historical but finds its explanation in his eschatological conceptions. He attributes to Yeshua the belief that he was the "Son of Man" mentioned in Daniel and that in order to appear again he must first be elevated to heaven, possibly through dying, and then come back: *"In order to understand Jesus' resolve to suffer, one must first recognize that the mystery of this suffering is involved in the mystery of the Kingdom of God, since that kingdom and along with it Jesus' Parousia cannot come until the great final tribulation have first taken place. For Jesus, suffering was always associated with the Messianic secret since he placed his Parousia at the end of the pre-Messianic tribulations in which he was to have his part. After the incident in Caesarea Philippi, the tribulation, as far as Jesus was concerned, was now connected with an historic event: he would go to Jerusalem and suffer death at the hands of the authorities. He didn't speak any more about the tribulations of others. They were abolished and concentrated upon himself alone. His new conviction was that he alone must suffer for others so that the kingdom might come. This change was due to the non-fulfillment of the predictions he had made in the discourse of sending forth the Twelve in mission. The cataclysm he expected had not occurred during their absence neither after their return. In leaving Galilea he abandoned the hope that the final tribulation would begin of itself. The movement of repentance had not been sufficient. God had decided otherwise in regard to the time of trial. He had eliminated the tribulation for others and Jesus was to alone undergo it; he was appointed to give his life for the many, the elect, to atone with his own blood the atonement that they would have had to render in the tribulation. He identified his condemnation and execution with the predicted pre-Messianic tribulations. Therefore, he set out for Jerusalem solely in order to die there, and once there provoked the authorities so that they would put him to death."*

It is clear that the Gospel writers tried to import elements of the old Testament into the New one; they attributed to Jesus the belief that Joel's, Daniel's and Isaiah's prophecies were to happen chronologically exactly as prophesized – tribulation, Messianic appearance, judgment, kingdom of God – and they applied that to him since they thought that he saw himself to be the Son of Man and the "suffering servant". We see here that A. Schweitzer, subscribing to this belief, also accepts the classical Pauline Christian belief that God made Yeshua suffer and die for the sake of others, and Yeshua decided to die in obedience to Him, a view repugnant to those who consider God as all-merciful and as the all-loving father of Yeshua. Was Yeshua accepted by his first disciples as a messiah claimant in the original Jewish sense of the word: a very religious powerful liberator from the foreign yoke, a kind of saintly leader claiming the throne of Israel, not a God-man, a would be God-king? In those days, the frontier between religion and life was inexistent. They envisioned everything as sacred; politics and religion were not divided. If the gospels say the truth about what Yeshua spoke, then he actually failed in what he allegedly believed his messianic mission was, and his main prophecy was not fulfilled. There is also a classic problem of Historic Jesus study which seems unavoidable, and that is the scholars creating a Jesus in their own image, a receptacle into which each one poured his own ideas, just like painters tend to unconsciously lend their own features to portraits.

My understanding

Under various strata of superstitions, dogmas and speculations, lies a simple truth. I am giving now a short sketch about Yeshua's life according to my understanding and various elements at our disposal. In around 4 or 6 BC, a special gentle soul took birth in the then-Roman province of Judea. He lived in his small village the simple life of the first son of a carpenter, with his three brothers, James, Jude or Judas Thomas (Judas the twin), Simon and two unnamed sisters – whose names can be gathered from other passages in the gospels as being Salome and Mary according to some people – until the age of twelve. After that followed a period during which nothing is known about him, at least not in the Christian sources collectively known as the New Testament. We can read in *Luke* 2:52 *"He kept on growing; his intelligence became more refined. He was pleasing God and men more and more."* That accounts for around twenty years.

According to the New Testament, when Yeshua was in his mid-thirties, he became an itinerant preacher. His cousin, John, was leading an ascetic life in the wild.[74] He had recently become an apocalyptic prophet and started to warn people about the soon-coming "Kingdom of God" and "Day of Judgement". He was a fiery preacher and preached the need for *metanoia*, inner transformation and a change of attitude, with repentance for one's sinful activities (*Mat.*3:2). He was offering people a ritual purification through baptism as a sign that they wanted to change their lives and so that God would forgive their sins (*Mark* 1:4; *Luke* 3:3). He was baptizing people – adults – in the waters of the Jordan river and had thus become known as the "Baptist". People would confess their sins publicly (*Mat.* 3:6) His baptism was not freeing people from their sins but was a sort of sacramental purification, in the sense that a sacrament creates a strong impression in the consciousness of people – a *samskara* in Vedic terms – helping them thereby to maintain their decision

---

[74] He was maybe a member of the mystic group called the Essenes, or a Nazarite, one consecrated to God for a period of time or for life, like Samson in *Judges* 13:5. Jesus did not observe the external rules of the Nazarite vow but he was clearly fully consecrated to God.

to lead a purer life and qualify for receiving the "Spirit".

In *Matthew*, when a group of Pharisees and Sadducees came once to receive baptism from him, John called them hypocrites and "vipers" and threatened them with fire and hell. He said the axe of God was near and all the trees giving bad fruits would be cut and burned; the Messiah was coming, he would harvest, keep the good grain and burn the husk in an everlasting fire. In *Luke*, he treated everyone of "vipers" and threatened everyone with hellfire (3:17). When Yeshua met John, he was baptized by him, and the Baptist allegedly[75] told the people who were around that his own role had been to prepare the venue of that same Yeshua, who would baptize not just with water but with the "Spirit" and fire. In *John* 1:29, the Baptist adds that it is Yeshua who would take the sins of the world, not God like in *Luke* 3:3 and *Mark* 1:4.

Yeshua gathered a group of disciples, some sent by John the Baptist from his own group, and started to preach the same message than John about the "Kingdom of God" or "Kingdom of Heaven" (*Mark* 1:15; *Mat*.4:17). From his discourses, it appears that he wanted to reform the religion he was born and raised in – Judaism – which had become reduced to rituals and dry formulas and had lost sight of its core teaching: love of God, what is known as *bhakti* in the Vedic spiritual tradition. He was stressing that love of God, for Whom he had developed a great filial love and Whom he called '*abba*', or 'father'. He was also preaching a very high ethic, a special type of righteousness beyond mere observance of the Mosaic Law, which he said was required to bring about the "Kingdom" and to be admitted into it. These ethical teachings, or practical application of the commandment to love one's next, were revolutionary in his day and age, what to speak of his spiritual message. He was very charismatic and attracted a lot of people. That made the Jewish

---

[75] It may be an interpolation meant to attract the Baptist's followers to the Jesus movement.

authorities jealous and worried, because his standards made them look bad in comparison and they were very attached to so many details of the Law while neglecting its essence. He publicly reproached it to them and they opposed him. Yeshua sent his disciples to preach the news of the coming Kingdom, telling them that they would meet a lot of tribulations and that they should be strong and determined, and also that before they would have gone through all the cities, they would see the "Son of Man" coming in glory to rule over the world and usher in the Kingdom. He kept preaching during their absence and a lot of people were coming to listen to him and followed him, as they were mostly peasants and village folks and the harvest season had passed, making them free.

But the months passed and the Kingdom did not come, and his disciples came back from their preaching tour. His mood then changed and he wanted to be alone with them but the crowds were following him around, even when he crossed the Jordan river. He personally distributed sanctified food (*prasadam* in the Vedic tradition) to those people on two occasions. Shortly after that, although the preaching was very successful, he told his disciples that he wanted to go to Jerusalem for the Passover. Yeshua was living in a country where people were miserable; they were praying for deliverance from the Roman oppression and were hoping for a deliverer. Various prophets had spoken that the end of the old world was soon coming. Many messiah claimants had risen before Yeshua, gathered a following and preached to people who were desperate and ready to follow anyone giving them hopes. They and their followers had been crushed by the political authorities.

Yeshua himself seemed to be moving in a world of apocalyptic thought, which was eschatological, completely impregnated with the idea that the "Kingdom of God" was near. He apparently thought he was the Messiah in whom all the people had hopes, but not in a political sense, it seems. It looks like he did not identify at all with a military victorious Messiah king but with the "suffering servant" Messiah" of Isaiah. In any case, it looks like he felt he was destined to play a major role in the advent of the "Kingdom of God", that he was even maybe ready to risk his life for the sake of his countrymen. He entered Jerusalem with his enthusiastic disciples. He had made himself the arrangement to enter the city sitting on an ass's colt as per prophet Zechariah's prophecy about the Messiah/king. His disciples were waving palms and hailing him. When people from the crowd asked who he was, they answered, "Yeshua, the prophet from Nazareth". He deliberately provoked the Jewish authorities by chasing away the merchants of animals destined for sacrificial offerings and the money changers, then haranguing the priests, scribes and Pharisees strongly, calling them all kinds of not so nice names. They decided to arrest him but not in front of the crowds who were enthusiastic about him, not to risk a riot.

Yeshua would preach in the temple courtyard during the day and would spend the night in a garden with his disciples just outside the city on Mount Olivet. During one night, although he was apparently ready to give his life to usher in the "Kingdom", he had prayed to his *abba* or father if death could nonetheless be spared to him but had surrendered to His divine will. That is what the *Gospel of Luke* (22:42) and of *Mark* (14:36) say, but there were no witnesses, all his disciples were asleep (*Luke* 22:45; *Mark* 14:36), so no one knows for sure. A few days before, he had told his disciples that if they did not have a sword they should sell their coat and buy one, and when he asked that evening how many they had and they answered two, he had said it was enough. (*Luke* 22:38) It seemed that he was waiting for a miracle to happen on that mount as had been prophesized; something like a symbolic fight would start and his *abba* would quickly send his angels to protect him, defeat his enemies and the "Kingdom" would come. However, this miracle did not happen when he was arrested very early in the morning by a troop of temple soldiers in arms. He was brought to the

Sanhedrin and was condemned to death. The Jewish court could pronounce a condemnation but depended upon the Romans for the death penalty. They told the governor, Pontius Pilatus, that Yeshua was a public agitator who had been preaching revolt in Judea and Galilea and had just come to Jerusalem to stir people there too. Pilatus spoke with him but allegedly did not find him guilty and did not want to have anything to do with him. The men of the Sanhedrin went into the crowd which was clamoring outside and told people that Yeshua had claimed to be the Messiah but that he was a fake. The crowds became angry, thinking he was another irresponsible Messiah claimant who would get them into trouble, so they asked Pilatus to crucify him.

So, under the pressure of the Jewish authorities and the crowd, he reluctantly agreed to condemn him. After just a few hours on the cross, he apparently died. A high-ranking member of the Sanhedrin, Joseph of Arimathea, who was favorable to Yeshua, asked his body to Pilatus and quickly had him brought down from the cross and taken to a nearby tomb he had recently bought. There Yeshua was healed, possibly by Essene healers. Some say that Joseph was an Essene himself. Yeshua was quickly taken away to a safe place to recover from the tremendous ordeal he had just been through. So there had not been a resurrection in the sense of him dying then coming back to life after a couple of days, but a loss of consciousness on the cross then a coming back to consciousness after sometimes once in the tomb.

He had been ready to sacrifice his life out of fidelity to the message he was preaching and to usher in the "Kingdom of God". He had prayed for a miracle but had fully surrendered to his father's will. He was crucified, but was spared death, thus tasting one of the fruits of his full surrender. His *abba* had heard him and loved him too much to allow his death for the sake of sinful people. *That* was the miracle. He was saved from death in spite of his readiness to die, or because of such readiness. But he was saved against his conscious will. In other words, he did not do anything to escape death but was saved. Another possible fruit of his full surrender is that if he did not bring the "Kingdom of God" on earth as he worked so hard for, he was himself taken to the Kingdom of God in the spiritual world. However, his disciples and followers did not know what truly happened. When he compassionately showed himself to them shortly after, before to disappear from the region never to be seen again there, they thought he had died and resurrected. That is what they preached even at the risk of their lives. Paul said during his preaching that if Jesus did not resurrect then his preaching was in vain and his audience's faith was in vain. Well, he did not know how right he was while writing that!

Chapter four
About the "Kingdom of God", Yeshua's failed core prediction.

The "Son of Man"

The Bible contains the claim that Israel had amongst its people many persons empowered or inspired by God to foresee the future and even perform miraculous feats. They are glorified in the Bible as very exalted people: the prophets. Their status as visionaries is taken as granted by the Christians and their gift is not questioned nor challenged. However, a close examination will reveal that they were not that gifted if they were at all, as many so-called prophecies were written after the events had happened – what is called post-diction, a Jewish literary device, a famous case of it being the prophecies posteriorly attributed to Daniel – and so many failed to happen. If the writers of the three earliest gospels are accurate in what they report Yeshua said, then, as many highly reputed biblical so-called "prophets" before him had been wrong in their predictions,[76] Yeshua was another "prophet" who was wrong in his main predictions. He claimed that he would come back and change the world within his own generation. Well, he did not directly say he would personally

---

[76] When the northern and southern kingdoms of Israel and Judea were respectively conquered in 722 BC by the Assyrians and destroyed in 586 BC by the Babylonians, Hosea, Isaiah, Jeremiah and Ezekiel promised the Jews that if they repented of their sins and worship of other gods, then their calamities which were sent by Yahweh as a punishment would stop and their land would be restored to them. But it did not happen in spite of the Jews following their advice. Isaiah claimed that Damascus would cease to be a city forever (17:1). It is the capital of Syria! He claimed that the Nile would dry up (19:5) but she never did! Ezekiel predicted that Nebuchadnezzar would destroy Tyra (26:7-14) but he didn't. He claimed that Egypt would become uninhabited and Egyptians would go into diaspora, which never happened. His prediction that Nebuchadnezzar would conquer Egypt (29:19) also proved wrong. Jeremiah wrote of a time when the Torah would be written in people' heart and that everyone would follow it. That didn't happen either.

come back; he said the "Son of Man" would appear. This term he used has been a topic of a lot of wondering and debate. Yeshua and the apostles spoke a Galilean dialect of Aramaic. Some scholars think that the mysterious expression *Bar-Nasha*, "the Son of Man", was merely a periphrasis for 'a man' or 'this man' or simply 'I'. It is only at a later time when Greek became the language of the Church that it was given an apocalyptic signification. The passages in the Gospel where it occurs in this sense are thus suspicious and to be put down to the account of early Christian theology. I am quoting here again the various opinions of German scholars found in A. Schweitzer's work.

Some of them, like Gustav Dalman in 1894, think that this expression was a veiling of Yeshua's Messiahship under a name which emphasizes the humanity of his bearer, a man par excellence, while actually implying that he was the man in whom Daniel's vision of "one like unto a Son of Man" was being fulfilled. A. Schweitzer thought that, *"Jesus used it when speaking of his Messiahship because it was the only way in which he could speak of it at all since his Messiahship was not yet realized but was only to be so at the appearing of the Son of Man. Only the initiated understood that he was speaking of his own coming, while others thought he spoke of the coming of someone else."*[77] But did Yeshua really assign that role to himself? It is unclear. In *Mark* 13:26 and *Luke* 12:8, for instance, or in *Matthew* 10:23, it really looks like he was speaking as the herald of someone else, someone identified with the messiah, of whom he was only the forerunner. Is it a term that he only used in those specific cases and that was then spread in all his utterings by the Evangelists, putting it in his mouth to "prove" that he was the Messiah foreseen by Daniel who used that term? Or did they simply put it in his mouth to "prove" so, without him ever using it? It has been generally assumed by the Christians since two thousand years that he meant himself by that term and that he was the Messiah, not his forerunner. Yeshua did change the world in some way, no

---

[77] *The Quest for the Historical Jesus*

doubt, but not at all in the way he had announced. An alternative explanation to Yeshua having been wrong would be that he did not refer to himself when he spoke of the coming of the "Son of Man". But even if we take as a possibility that it did not mean himself, that "Son of Man" did not appear either, nor did he perform what Yeshua had announced. The events which he predicted that his disciples would witness simply never happened. The world continued to exist and did not change. So he was proved wrong by history.

The Messianic kingdom

The Jewish religion is a group affair; they always speak about "the people". In Antiquity, the group had priority on the individual. Even Socrates refused his friends' offer to make Him escape from jail and death for not causing disrepute to the group he belonged to, the city of Athens. Although Yeshua brought about the consciousness of the individual, valorizing not a mass religion consisting in rituals and ostentatious worship but the religion of a personal relationship of love with God, he was basically preaching to people as a group to repent and to believe that the "Kingdom of God" was at hand. His ethics are the ethics of virtue, goodness, a necessary platform for elevation of consciousness. That is why it was so difficult for the people to understand him, his disciples included, as they were mostly under the influence of passion and ignorance, and his teachings require goodness, virtue, to be understood and applied. Later, Christians have mostly focalized on the ethics he preached, thinking they were saved by his alleged vicarious atonement for their sins and did not need an intense inner spiritual life. Except the spiritualists, of course.

The ethical dimension of Yeshua's message was subordinate to that: one should not just follow the Mosaic law but develop a higher righteousness, a deeper moral, to purify oneself and thereby attract the advent of the "kingdom". Such a belief in a future Messianic kingdom existed long before John the Baptist's preaching but he and Yeshua actualized it, making it for the people something tangible soon to manifest. In Pharisaic thinking, the kingdom of God had two meanings: it meant the present kingdom or reign of God, or it could mean the future reign of God all over the world in the Messianic age. Yeshua frequently used the same expression with the same twofold meaning: sometimes a present kingdom *"The kingdom of God is among you"*, sometimes a future kingdom, *"Repent for the kingdom of God is near."* So the idea that the kingdom would come at the end of times floated among the people, but that end was now announced as due to happen anytime soon, at least within the generation of Yeshua and his audience.

"I will come back!"

The evidence about Yeshua's failed prophecy has been hotly debated in vain ever since by Christian apologists and theologians who try to wiggle some other meaning out of it because his reliability is at stake. But, however difficult to stomach because they did not happen, his claims as recorded in the three synoptic gospels are very clear and straightforward, with no room for interpretation: He promised the coming of the "Son of Man" and the "Kingdom of God" to his disciples before the end of the existing generation. The author of *John* later also mentioned Yeshua's promise to come back, but without giving any details: *"I won't leave you alone like orphans. I will come back among you"* (14:18); *"I told you I will come back"* (14:28); *"You will see me again soon"* (16:18); *"I will come back to see you soon"* (16:22). Let us review what the first three Gospels say: In *Matthew* Yeshua sends his preachers all over the country to proclaim that the Messiah is bringing the "Kingdom of God" (10:5-43), giving them warnings about all kinds of terrible things which will happen to them and tells them, *"When you are persecuted in one place, flee to another. I tell you the truth, you will not finish going through the cities of Israel before the Son of Man comes"* (10:23). After we do not know exactly how much time, the preachers come back but have not been persecuted at all and the mysterious "Son of Man" has not appeared. A possible explanation is that the text of *Mark* does not present events in a chronological order, as written by Papias of Hierapolis (c 60-163) citing John the Elder, *"Mark wrote down as many things as he recalled from memory – though not in an ordered form – of the things either said or done by Jesus that he had heard from Peter, who used to give his teachings in the form of short anecdotes but had no intention of providing an ordered arrangement of the logia of the Lord."* So this preaching tour maybe does not appear in its proper place or the passage consists of two anecdotes or more which have been arbitrarily joined together.

Anyway, later on, after having announced to his disciples the impending destruction of the temple, saying that, *"not one stone will be left here upon another; all will be thrown down"*, Yeshua describes in great detail on the Mount Olivet the signs which will show that the great tribulation preceding that destruction has begun, as well as the suffering they will undergo at that time. He tells them clearly that when they see the *"abomination that causes desolation"*, which in apocalyptic language refers to the desecration of the temple by the Romans – as it had been in 176 BC by the Seleucid king Antiochus IV Epiphanes who had a pig sacrificed to Zeus in it and outlawed Yahweh's worship, an incident which instigated the Maccabean revolt – they should flee and regroup in the mountains, as David had done and as Mattathias Maccabee and his sons had done. They should wait there until the temple is destroyed; then immediately after that, as described by Isaiah about Babylon, by Ezekiel about the destruction of Egypt, as well as in Daniel's prophecies, it will be "the day of Yahweh" and *"the Son of Man, will come back with great power and glory"*. Yeshua, although very clear in his predictions of what would happen and that it was imminent, told them that some of them would still be alive when that would happen, but admitted that he did not know exactly when that would happen, but only his Father did.[78] This is not an escape clause, as Thom Stark calls it with humor in *The Human Faces of*

---

[78] *Mark* 13:32; *Matt* 24:36

God; this is not either (as misinterpreted by many Christians) a statement that this would happen at some indefinite time in the distant future, but a clear unambiguous declaration that it would be within this generation; he just did not know exactly when that would be during that time frame.

The expectation Yeshua had expressed for the imminent happening of events which did not happen has led one more former evangelist preacher turned atheist – John W. Loftus – to write, "*At best Jesus was a failed apocalyptic prophet.*"[79] Thom Stark writes, "*I do not see coming to the point of being able to say that Jesus himself was wrong as a choice between faith and reason, but as a choice between blind faith and reasonable faith. A reasonable faith is mature enough to acknowledge when it needs to be corrected and it can survive such corrections. In fact, a mature faith learns to thrive on them.*" According to this remark of Stark about faith and J.W. Loftus' own admission, the latter's former faith in Christianity was obviously more blind than reasonable. But his doubts led him to investigate the case more deeply, and his approach became so reasonable that he could not believe anymore something which he understood to be flawed at the core for lack of sufficient evidence, such as Bible stories not being confirmed by archeology but infirmed by it, the Bible being inconsistent with itself, its containing fairy tales, rewritings of former texts with alterations, failed prophecies and forgeries. But if the Gospels are to be trusted on that particular point, it seems that not even a great soul like Yeshua was immune to fallibility. Then we have to conjecture that probably because of the apocalyptic vision of the world that he had inherited by taking birth at that place and time in history, he had the expectation that he expressed for an imminent happening of events which did not happen. It seems that he thought that he was the latest prophet in the line, and so he is portrayed as having equated allegiance to himself with allegiance to God, believing that his brand of Judaism was the one which could save

---

[79] *The Christian Delusion: Why Faith Fails.*

the Jews from destruction and the imminent judgment. He was apparently waiting for a miracle to make a spiritual revolution happen. His hopes were not fulfilled. He was proved wrong by the course of events.[80]

From the Vedic point of view, if Yeshua did not reach full self-realization before leaving his body, his expected "second coming" was simply in the form of his reincarnating somewhere else under another name and being not recognized. He may have reincarnated, but that is not what the predictions of "the Son of Man" coming back *with power and glory* indicated. In any case, his core prediction was wrong. Obviously, neither he neither the "Son of Man", if that was a different person, did perform what he said he would. There is no way to maneuver around that. That presents Christianity with a formidable problem: The supreme object of their faith was wrong, and so far two thousand years wrong.

Various interpretations

Yeshua was always talking about that "Kingdom of God", or "Kingdom of heaven" in *Matthew*. The expression comes back ninety-nine times in the Gospels. But what is the nature of that kingdom? It is presented in a paradoxical way as we just saw, as being already present (*Luke* 11:20) and yet as to be coming in the future (in the Lord's prayer)! And also as being near, at hand (*Luke* 19:9), and at the same time as being far away, far off (*Luke* 19:11)! Moreover, Yeshua described the signs of the coming of the kingdom (*Luke* 21:5-36) while affirming to his disciples that they could not figure out when it would come, that only God knew, that neither the angels nor himself knew when!? The apocalyptic import of Yeshua talking about that kingdom was maybe clear for the people he was preaching to, but it is not certain because the author of *Mark* wrote, "*That kingdom is a*

---

[80] James Dunn, *Jesus Remembered* P. 479

mysterious secret" (4:10). The problem is that nobody really knows now what Yeshua meant by the "Kingdom". Is it because we do not have any clear explanation about it given in the New Testament?

[The German scholar Hermann Samuel Reimarus (1694-1768) reasoned that, *"The Kingdom of God must be understood according to Jewish ways of thought since neither John the Baptist nor Jesus ever explained clearly the expression, so it means that both were content to have it understood according to its known and customary sense. The catechism and confession of the early Church was simple. Belief was not difficult: They needed only to believe the good news that Jesus was about to bring in the Kingdom of God. This was the sum total of what his disciples knew about it when they were sent out by their master to proclaim its coming. Their hearers would naturally think of the customary meaning of the term and the hopes attached to it. The Gospel therefore meant nothing more or less that under his leadership the Kingdom of God was about to be brought in. To gain a historical understanding of Jesus' teachings, we must leave behind what we learned in our catechism about the metaphysical Divine Son-ship, the Trinity and similar dogmatic conceptions and go out in a wholly Jewish world of thought. Only those who carry the catechism back into the Jewish messiah's preaching will arrive at the idea that he was the founder of a new religion. To all unprejudiced persons, it is manifest that Jesus had not the slightest intention of doing away with Judaism and putting another religion in its place. It's only in Jesus' insistence on a new and deeper morality and righteousness, a requisite for the Kingdom of God, that his preaching went beyond the ideas of his contemporaries. But this new morality didn't do away with the Law, for he explained it as the fulfillment of the old commandments. The only change Jesus made in the religion is that the expected messiah was already present. On the cross, Jesus cried out loud to God, 'Why have you abandoned me?' This avowal cannot be interpreted without violence to the text otherwise than as meaning that God* had not aided Him in his aim and purpose as he had hoped. That shows that it had not been his purpose to suffer and die, but to establish an earthly Kingdom of God and deliver the Jews from political oppression, and in that God's help had failed him. For his disciples, this turn of affairs meant the destruction of all the dreams for the sake of which they had followed him – that they would take their places as the friends and ministers of the messiah, as the judges and rulers of the twelve tribes of Israel. Jesus never disabused them of this sensuous hope, but confirmed them in it when they were quarrelling about preeminence. All this implies that the time of the fulfillment of their hopes was not thought of by him and by them as at all remote.

In 1863, Heinrich J. Holtzmann wrote that, "*Jesus had endeavored in Galilea to found the kingdom of God in an ideal sense. He concealed his consciousness of being the Messiah to his disciples until the end of his Galilean tour, when he declared to them in Caesarea Philippi that he was the Messiah. He decided to put the Messianic cause to the test in Jerusalem. The indifference of the people and the hatred of the priestly hierarchy extremely tenacious of their claims and equally sensitive to their infringement, endowed with hearts in which there was no room for love, a morality inwardly riddled with decay, an outward show of virtue and a hypocritical arrogance, let no doubts about the issue of the confrontation.*" He was of the opinion that the theory that Yeshua predicted a personal, bodily Second Coming in the brightness of his heavenly splendor and surrounded by the heavenly hosts to establish an earthly kingdom is not only not proved but is absolutely impossible. For him, Yeshua's purpose was to establish a community of which his disciples are the foundation, and by means of this community to bring about the coming of the Kingdom of God.

Timothée Colani wrote in 1864 that, "*A spiritual conception of the Kingdom of God could not be combined with the thought of a glorious Second Coming.*" He rejected as later interpolations the words of Yeshua forecasting the coming of the "Son of Man" before the disciples would have finished preaching in all the cities of Israel (*Matt.*10:23), the promise of twelve thrones on which they would judge the twelve tribes of Israel (possibly a later interpolation made to give a lot of authority to those twelve in the budding Church), the saying about his return before the death of the disciples present (*Matt.*23:39) and his claim to the Council that he will come on the clouds of heaven (*Matt.* 24) . Karl T. Keim in 1867 said that, "*A Kingdom of God clothed with material splendors formed an integral part of Jesus' preaching from the first; he never rejected it and therefore never by a so-called advance transformed the sensuous Messianic idea into a purely spiritual one. He did not uproot from the minds of the sons of Zebedee their beliefs in the thrones on his right hand and his left... It is impossible that Jesus can have thought of himself as the judge of the world, for the Jewish and Jewish-Christian eschatology does not ascribe the conduct of the Last Judgment to the Messiah. That was first done by Gentile Christians, and especially by Paul. It was therefore the later eschatology which set the Son of Man on the throne of his glory and prepared the twelves thrones of judgment for the disciples.*"

Wilhelm Baldensperger in 1888 wrote that, "*In the time of Jesus a fully formed Messianic expectation existed with a many-sided growth. It is self-evident that Jesus' conception of the Kingdom of God had a double character, that the eschatological and spiritual elements were equally represented in it and mutually conditioned one another, and that Jesus therefore began, in pursuance of this conception, to found a spiritual invisible Kingdom, although he expected its fulfillment to be effected by supernatural means. Jesus had rejected the ideal of the Messianic king of David's line and put away all warlike thoughts. Then he began to found the Kingdom of God by preaching. His silence regarding his Messianic office was partly due to the fact that he wanted to lead his hearers to a more spiritual conception of the kingdom and so to obviate a possible political action on their part and the consequent intervention of the Roman government. Prior to the confession at Caesarea Philippi, the disciples had only a faint and vague suspicion of the Messianic dignity of their master. Jesus wondered whether the people would accept him as messiah. He put the question to them in Jerusalem in all its sharpness and burning actuality, and the people were moved to enthusiasm. But as soon as they saw that he whom they had hailed with such acclamation was neither able nor willing to fulfill their ambitious dreams, a reaction set in. Thus there was an interaction between the historical and the psychological events."*

A. Schweitzer wrote that, *"Johann Weiss in 1892 laid down the third great alternative that the study of the life of Jesus had to meet. The first was laid won by Strauss: either purely historical or purely supernatural. The second had been worked out by the Tübingen school and Holtzmann: either Synoptic or Johannine. Now came the third: either eschatological or non-eschatological. Progress always consist in taking one or other of two alternatives, in abandoning the attempt to combine them. Weiss rightly grasped the general conception of the Kingdom of God. He insisted that all modern ideas, even in their subtlest forms must be eliminated from it. When this is done, we arrive at a Kingdom of God which is wholly future. Being still to come, it is at present purely supra-mundane. Jesus doesn't establish it. He only proclaims its coming. He exercises no Messianic functions, but waits like others for God to bring about the coming of the kingdom by supernatural means. He doesn't even know the day and hour when this shall come to pass. The missionary journey of the disciples was only a means of rapidly and widely making known its nearness. But it was not so near as Jesus thought. The impenitence and hardness of heart of a great part of the people, and the implacable enmity of his opponents at length convinced him that the establishment of the Kingdom of God could not yet take place, that such penitence as had been shown hitherto was not sufficient, and that a mighty obstacle, the guilt of the people, must first be put away. It becomes clear to him that his own death must be the ransom-price.*

So Weiss clings to the idea that Yeshua gave his life to save the Jews from the weight of their sins so that there would not be anymore an obstacle to the coming of the Kingdom of God. That is a Pauline idea inserted later on in the teachings of the early Church then extended to all men. *"After his death he would come again in all the splendor and glory with which, since the days of Daniel, men's imaginations had surrounded the Messiah, and he was to come, moreover, within the lifetime of the generation to which he had proclaimed the nearness of the Kingdom of God. This Kingdom had nothing whatever to do with political expectations. Jesus didn't preach a special ethic of the kingdom but only an ethic which in this world makes men free from the world and prepared to enter unimpeded into the kingdom. That is why his ethic is of so completely negative a character; it is in fact not so much an ethic as a penitential discipline. The Messiahship claimed by Jesus is not a present office; its exercise belongs to the future. On earth, he is only a man, a prophet. 'Son of Man', is therefore in the passages where it is authentic, a purely eschatological designation of the Messiah, though we cannot tell whether his hearers understood him as speaking of himself in his future rank and dignity, or whether they thought of the Son of Man as being quite distinct from himself, whose coming he was only proclaiming in advance. The Messianic self-consciousness of Jesus, as expressed in the title 'Son of Man', shares in the transcendental apocalyptic character of Jesus' idea of the kingdom of God and cannot be separated from that idea."*

A. Schweitzer wrote, *"So Weiss asserted like Ghillany thirty years earlier but on a scientifically unassailable basis that the part played by Jesus was not the active role of establishing the kingdom but the passive role of waiting for the coming of the kingdom. Jesus seems to have been convinced that the coming of the Kingdom of God was near at hand. Why then did he feel the need to preach a social ethic? Precisely to accelerate the coming of the Kingdom of God. He believed that the individual had to purify himself. But why did one need to purify oneself to enter a kingdom on earth?*

Because there would be the Judgement. It seems the Kingdom of God was a mixture of an earthly place and a spiritual inner place in communion with God... Actually, we are unable to discover what the mystery of the Kingdom of God in Mark 4 is, any more than we can understand why it must be veiled, and we must number it among the unsolved problems of Jesus' preaching of the Kingdom... Jesus had been surprised that in his hometown there were so few believers, that is so few elect, as he thought that the Kingdom of God could appear at any moment. He plainly told the Twelve that he did not expect to see them back after their preaching tour in the present age (Matt. 10:23) because the Parousia of the 'Son of Man', which is logically and temporally identical with the dawn of the Kingdom, would take place before they would come back from their tour. The whole of his discourse to them is a prediction of the events of the "time of the end", which Jesus thought were immediately at hand. It was part of the preaching of the approach of the Kingdom of God. Jesus seems to have thought that his Parousia would happen during his lifetime, which means that he would be transported first supernaturally to heaven, then come down again from it transformed, in glory.][81]

Let us be simple!

Maybe the simplest explanation is the best, like the principle of Ockham's razor in science. I personally believe that Yeshua always had a spiritual conception of the Kingdom of God. He described it as something living, a process of becoming, growing in the consciousness of the faithful until it would be reached. He was dealing with very down-to-earth people; they had no other-worldly conception of the "Kingdom of God". As an empowered preacher of love of God, he simply chose to use the pre-existent belief in the "Kingdom", as well as peoples' mundane hopes for it to come soon, to try to convince them to stop sinning and repent, in order to elevate them to a higher standard. He meant to make

---

[81] *The Quest for the Historical Jesus*

them go deeper, go beyond the mere religious platform to the spiritual one, which means developing a personal relationship with God not based on the group and fear of the law but on love. That would take them to the "Kingdom" which is both inside of the heart of the believer on the way to it and beyond him as he has not reached it yet. He thus "played the game" of the bearer of the good news that the "Kingdom of God" was coming, for the masses and his disciples; then, after they got attached to him and were somewhat purified, he raised the bar higher and spoke words that those who were ready to hear could understand to mean that the "Kingdom of God" was actually not to be looked for on earth, externally, but one could access it within oneself if one raised his consciousness and developed one's personal relationship of love with God.

As we saw, Yeshua let his disciples believe until the end that they would have thrones to sit on to judge and rule the people after his coming back in glory. Was it a preaching tactic? I think so. And it worked, because in any case they took him literally, believing that an earthly Jewish Kingdom was about to manifest, where there would not be anymore any oppression from the dreaded and hated Romans and where they, as Jews, would show the world that they were indeed the chosen people of God and all the kings of the nations would come and pay tribute to their messiah King.

That corresponds well to the Jewish mentality; so much so that, as late as the 17th century, when Shabbataï Tsevi claimed in Turkey to be the Messiah then moved with his followers to Jerusalem, the hopes of the Jews of the diaspora swelled. In the Yemenite capital, Sanaa, for instance, convinced that they would become the rulers, they started to behave boldly with the Muslims, something they had never dared to do previously in their condition of humiliated, abused "inferiors", *dhimmis*. In their feverish minds they decided that the Muslims should abdicate the political power in their favor. They even chose among themselves a governor and went in procession with him to ask the local emir to submit and give them the keys of the town. That amazed so much the emir that he had their "governor" examined to see if he was sane and not under the influence of some intoxicating substance. He then got him jailed up and reported the case to the imam, who was so infuriated that he had the "governor" killed and his corpse suspended at the gate of the town; then he multiplied by twenty the *jizia* tax on non-Muslims and had their wealth confiscated for years. His successor had their synagogues razed to the ground. To add insult to injury, the news came that the so-called messiah had converted to Islam to save his neck from the Turkish sultan. The Jews were banned from the town and escorted in the desert, a long Calvary during which so many died. Later, they were allowed to come back. [82]

"Moving back the goal posts"

Although Yeshua's core prophecy, as it has been usually interpreted, has thus been proved to be dead wrong, curiously, his cult survived. How? As far as the early Christians are concerned, it seems that after many a long year had passed, the temple had been destroyed but the Romans had not been crushed, disillusionment ensued among them. People were mocking and scoffing at their unfulfilled expectations. Themselves were desperately looking for some explanation to the undue delay and the embarrassing and disheartening reality. They were adapting and reconfiguring their upset expectations by squeezing away the imminence of the Parousia. In other words, they were "moving back the goal posts", to use John Loftus' terms. Disappointments gave birth to adjustments. Paul seems to have thought he would see the end of the world, the *eschaton*, happening during his own lifetime. When it did not happen after many years of preaching, he wrote (*Romans*) that God had heartened the Jews' hearts so the *eschaton* was delayed until enough Gentiles would be saved through his preaching. But

---

[82] Ali Al-Muqri, *Le beau Juif*, Liana Levi, 2011

his death came, not the kingdom...In *Mark*, the destruction of the temple was supposed to be the sign that Yeshua was coming back. Since the temple had been destroyed and Yeshua had not come back, the Gospel writers after *Mark* started to make adjustments. The author of *Matthew* altered the narration found in *Mark* and had the disciples asking Yeshua what would be the sign that he would be coming back very soon. *Luke*, which was written even later, when all the disciples had already died, mentions that "*the people were thinking that the kingdom of God would appear at once*" (19:11). It does not mention Yeshua coming back with power like in *Mark*. To cover up the failure of the prophecy which had still not concretized itself by the time he was writing, the author of *John* does not even speak about Yeshua coming back but about the "coming of the Holy Spirit"– as if the presence of the Holy Spirit, who is already in the heart of every living being, was something especially reserved to the apostles.

Revelation was apparently written during Nero's reign. The end was supposed to come during those times. As it did not, the text was later edited to make the *eschaton* to come during the reign of Domitian. It did not, so the subsequent Christian writers kept on negotiating and reconstructing its coming through allegorical and metaphorical interpretations, among which was that one day of the Lord is like one thousand human years. Another one was replacing the earthly "Kingdom of God" with an otherworldly one.[83] So one replacement idea spread: the kingdom, the coming of which Yeshua clearly predicted would manifest on earth any day, is not actually on earth but in heaven and one should prepare during one's whole life to be taken there. As I mentioned, I think that Yeshua preached allegorically and that this "replacement idea" is actually the proper understanding. Other popular ideas emerged in time because of

---

[83] *John* 18:36

the delay in the advent of the "Kingdom": one is that the "Kingdom" was the Roman empire after the emperors had converted to Christianity; this was claimed by Constantine and later by Justinian. Another one is that the "Kingdom" was the Church itself, a dominant Catholic belief from the 4th century to the 20th. We can observe that many modern apocalyptic Christian movements, in which a precise date had been given for the coming of the "Kingdom" and that date has arrived but not the "Kingdom", have also survived. This is because, as the early Christians and all Christians ever since, they have reinterpreted the failed prophecy from hindsight, desperately clinging to their false belief and hope rather than questioning and reconsidering the whole "myth".

The first Jewish Christians took – and Christians ever since take – the preaching of Yeshua about the "Kingdom" literally. That is why it can be safely said that his prophecy was a failure from this point of view. Another alternative explanation is that the gospels do not contain reliable testimony about Jesus, which presents Christianity with a formidable problem. How has Christianity survived such a failure? In 1830, August Gfrörer described Christianity as a system which now only maintains itself by the force of custom, after having commanded itself to antiquity by the hope of the mystic Kingdom of the future world and having ruled the Middle Ages by the fear of the same future. The Christians have been reinterpreting the failed prophecy ever since from hindsight. But such a stop-gap measure should not have been enough, even for people of blind or sentimental faith. Is it because Christianity became the only religion permitted in the empire from the fourth century on? Well, it is said that many so-called heretics took shelter of the desert of Arabia, which probably meant the Nabatean kingdom of Petra and other oases. But it is true that to leave everything and exile oneself in the desert, at the term of a dangerous journey, was an extreme move limited to a relatively small number of people. I think that the problem of the failed prophecy was actually completely dwarfed by Paul's claim that Yeshua willingly died for the sins of all mankind. Indeed, if that was the case, who really cares if Jesus was wrong on the other hand like all doomsday prophets have ever been? The hope or conviction that one has achieved freedom from one's sinful reactions and is thus "saved" would make one overlook such a "mistake". I believe that this is what happened.

In Catholicism, the future coming back of Yeshua ushering the "kingdom of God" is an article of faith in the Creed – *"May Thy kingdom come"* – but hardly anyone speaks about it nor bothers. Among the Protestants, on the other hand, it is very much a prominent thought. Some even express their yearning for the "rapture", their elevation in their present body to meet Yeshua coming back in glory in mid-air, another absurd invention found in Paul's writings: *"The Lord himself will come down from heaven with a cry of command, the voice of an archangel and the sound of the trumpet of God. And the dead in Christ will rise first. Then we who are alive, who are left, will be caught up together with them in the clouds to meet the Lord in the air, and so we will always be with the Lord."* (1*Thes.*4:16-17)

The alternative explanation to Yeshua having been wrong is that even if he did refer to himself when he used the terms "the Son of Man coming in glory and power with the angels", this was just a preaching tactic to keep his disciples "on the edge" so that they would remain eager, purify themselves and not become slack. Yet another alternative explanation is that the gospels do not contain reliable testimony about Yeshua's claims: he never actually said the words later attributed to him. He never pronounced those according to which "the Son of Man" would come before they would have preached in all the cities of Israel, nor those according to which some of his disciples would still be alive when the same "Son of Man" would come back accompanied by angels, judge mankind and usher in the utopia of the "Kingdom of God". We then have to deny that he thought himself to be the Messiah; we need then to regard the idea that he thought he was as a later interpolation by the writers of the Gospels attributing these Messianic claims to Yeshua because the belief of the early Jewish Christian and Christian communities was that he was the Messiah. That presents Christianity with an equally formidable problem. Either their worshipable Yeshua/Jesus was another failed prophet, either they misunderstood his allegorical teachings, either the Gospels are unreliable and he was not the Messiah. If the Gospels are not reliable, then the basis for Christianity is inexistent. Is Christianity then resting upon a fraud and did not grow out of Yeshua's teachings but is a later creation based on speculations and interpretations!? But there is an itch: it does not sound convincing that Yeshua did not pronounce those words. From what we have been told for two millennia, his disciples and the newcomers to his movement after his crucifixion, as well as Paul and his converts, were all expecting to see within their own lifetime the Parousia, the imminent end of the world as it was and its regeneration, as per his clear statements. That informed Paul's moral instructions and his stance on marriage as an entanglement distracting believers from fully dedicating themselves to preparing the way for the "Kingdom of God" which was supposed to come anytime soon. That belief was pervasive among all the followers of Yeshua. Thus it seems that he did pronounce those words. So, is John Loftus right? Was Yeshua a failed apocalyptic prophet in the sense that his preaching tactic worked so well that everybody took literally his words? That can make him seen as a not fully reliable religious authority, notwithstanding the value of his ethic teachings and his preaching about love of God...Or is there something which escapes us? And if so, is it because it has been omitted by the writers of the Gospels, or later edited off? Or are these passages, on the contrary, later interpolations?

Christian H. Weisse tried to get rid of the problem by the following device. He wrote in 1838, "*In speaking of the Parousia of the 'Son of Man', Jesus was using a figure which includes in a mysterious fashion all his predictions of the future. He did not speak to his disciples of his resurrection, ascension and Parousia as three distinct acts since the event to which he looked forward is not identical to any of the three but is composed of them all: The resurrection is at the same time the ascension and Parousia, and in the latter the two formers are also included. The personal presence of Jesus which his disciples experienced after his death was in their view only a partial fulfillment of that general promise. The Parousia appeared to them as still awaiting fulfillment."*

Karl T. Keim also tried to wiggle away from the difficulty. He rightfully wrote in 1867 that the conduct of the disciples after the death of Yeshua forbids us to suppose that the Resurrection had been predicted in clear and unambiguous sayings. But then he goes on, *"The announcements of the Second Coming coincide in point of time with the predictions of the Resurrection, and the predictions both of the Second Coming and of the Resurrection stand in organic connection with the announcement of his approaching death. The two are therefore identical. It was only after his death that the disciples differentiated the thought of the Resurrection from that of the Second Coming. The spiritual presence of their master who had manifested himself did not seem to them to be the fulfillment of the promise of the Second Coming."* The question indeed in that case is that concerning the identity or difference of the Parousia and the Resurrection. Karl Keim hoped that perhaps a way could be found of causing the "error" of Yeshua to disappear and proving it to have been an illusion due to the want of a sufficiently close study of his discourses. Some scholars thought that the expectation of the Parousia in the sensuous form in which it meets us in the documents, is due to a misunderstanding of Yeshua's teachings on the part of his disciples. Others maintained that it was an integral part of his teachings. August Gfrörer did not believe that Yeshua himself thought that he was to rise from the dead. Nevertheless, the 'resurrection' is historic in the sense that He was brought back to consciousness in the tomb by Joseph of Arimathea.[84]

---

[84] *The Quest for the Historical Jesus*

Chapter five
About the resurrection

Apparently, Jesus was seen alive by his disciples after his crucifixion and burial, and it seems that these were not hallucinations. His tomb was found empty, although strangely enough Paul does not mention such a good preaching argument. He does not mention anything anyway about the life of the historical Yeshua, except the resurrection. The Jews do not accept the resurrection and call it a myth. In the Talmud it is mentioned, *"Yeshu later went to the Jerusalem Temple...On a day before the Passover, they hanged him on a tree... and he was buried. His followers on Sunday told that he was not in his grave, that he ascended to heaven as he had prophesied. As a gardener took him from the grave, they searched it and could not find him. But the gardener confessed he had taken it to prevent his followers from stealing his body and claiming his ascension to heaven."*[85] This story was apparently known before the resurrection stories were incorporated into the canonical gospels,[86] as these gospels are keen to explain away the story by the improbable claim that guards were bribed to claim that the body had been stolen while they slept (*Matt.* 28:11-15). The Muslims do not accept either the resurrection of Yeshua because the Koran states that he was not crucified or that he did not die to begin with: *"They boasted, 'We killed Christ Jesus, the son of Mary, the Messenger of Allah.' But they did not kill him, nor crucified him, but so it was made to appear to them...for a surety they did not kill him. No, Allah raised him unto Himself* (4.157-8).

---

[85] Van Voorst Robert E. *Jesus Outside the New Testament: An Introduction to the Ancient Evidence.* Wm B Eerdmans Publishing. 2000 p 123-6.

[86] There is no mention of the resurrection in the oldest manuscripts of Mark. They only appear in it around 200AD.

According to this passage, either God's power of illusion made it appear that he died but he did not; he was then put in a tomb which was found empty because God healed him or took him to heaven, where he continues to live until his return in the "second coming"; either someone was substituted to him and crucified: one of his followers took his place. Tony Bushby in *The Bible Fraud* claims that Simon of Cyrene was the one who volunteered to be crucified instead of Yeshua. This is not a new idea. In the early second century, Basilides of Alexandria had claimed that Yeshua had not died upon the cross. As there is no evidence for this theory in the canonical gospels, he wrote a whole new gospel of his own that he attributed to Simon Peter himself, who allegedly transmitted this secret *gnosis* denied to less enlightened Christians. Yeshua had swapped his body with Simon of Cyrene and Simon was crucified in his stead. Thinking about it, that could be a good explanation of the whole resurrection mystery: Yeshua appeared again to his disciples after the crucifixion of his substitute, not his own...

The German scholar Reimarus' treatment of the resurrection is quite original. [He wrote around 1750 with great logic that the disciples were prepared for anything rather than that which actually happened; that Yeshua had never told a word to his disciples about his dying and rising again, otherwise it is completely illogical that they would have played the coward at his death or that they would have been so astonished and incredulous at his reappearance. The three or four sayings referring to these events must therefore have been put into his mouth later, in order to make it appear that he had foreseen these events in his original plan. How did they get over this devastating blow? Until then, their thoughts, as Yeshua's, had been dominated by the eschatological idea of the prophets – the scion of David who should appear as the political deliverer of the nation. But there was another Messianic expectation which transferred everything to the supernatural sphere, appearing first in Daniel: The Messiah is to appear twice, once in human lowliness, the second time upon the clouds of heaven. When the first form of Messiahship failed, annihilated by Yeshua's untimely and unexpected death, they fell back on the second form of Messianic hope. They gave his death the significance of a spiritual redemption, which had not previously entered neither their field of vision neither Yeshua's. But that spiritual interpretation would not have helped them if they had not also...invented the resurrection. They were first in deadly fear to be searched after and condemned like their master, but when one or two slipped out of their hiding place they found out that nothing of the sort was going on. So they stole the body of Yeshua and hid it. After prudently waiting fifty days in order that the body, if it should be found, would be unrecognizable, they proclaimed to the people that Yeshua had resuscitated, that they had seen him and talked to him, that he had been elevated to heaven from which he would soon return.

That hope of the Parousia was the fundamental thing in early Christianity, which appears to be a product of that hope more than of Yeshua's teachings. Accordingly, the main problem of primitive dogmatics was the delay of that Parousia. Paul was working to discover all possible and impossible reason why it should be delayed and was obliged to fob people off somehow or other. The author of *2 Peter* came up with the sophism of 1000 years which are one day in the sight of God, forgetting that Yeshua had promised to return by man's years not by God's. But nonetheless, the Christians of later generations, including Fathers of the Church continue ever after to feed themselves with empty hopes. The theologians of the present day skim over the eschatological material in the Gospels because it doesn't chime in with their views, but inasmuch as the non-fulfilment of its eschatology is not admitted, Christianity rests upon a fraud. No miracle would prove that 2 and 2 make 5 or that a circle has 4 angles; and no miracles, however numerous, could remove a contradiction which lies on the surface of teachings and records of Christianity. Nor is there any weight in the appeal to the fulfillment of prophecy, for the cases in which the author of Matthew countersigns it with the words 'that the Scriptures be fulfilled' are all artificial and unreal. The sole argument which could save the credit of Christianity would be a proof that the

Parousia really took place at the time for which it was announced, but obviously no such proof can be produced.

Two other German writers of roughly the same era, Karl Friedrich Bahrdt in 1782 and the theologian Karl Heinrich Venturini in 1800, wrote fictitious lives of Yeshua, attempting to apply with logical consistency a non-supernatural interpretation to the miracle stories of the Gospel. Bahrdt thought he had found the key to the explanation of Yeshua's life in the person of Nicodemus and Joseph of Arimathea who make a late but significant appearance in the Gospels. He wrote that they were not Yeshua's disciples but Essenes. This Order had members in all ranks of society including the Sanhedrin. It had set itself the task of detaching the nation from its material Messianic hopes and leading it to a higher knowledge of spiritual truths. In order to deliver the people from the limitations of the national faith in an earthly Messiah, which could only lead to disturbances and insurrection as it had done so far, they needed a person to play the part of a Messiah who would destroy these false Messianic expectations. They noticed Yeshua during his youth and taught him to enter deeper and deeper into the knowledge of wisdom over the years. In the beginning of his ministry, Yeshua appeared in the role of the Messiah of popular expectation and worked by means of miracles and illusions, helped by the medicine he had been given and by the clever Essenes. An apparent death and resurrection was part of the plan to spiritualize people' conception of the Messiah. Yeshua provoked the authorities by his triumphal Messianic entry and chasing the merchants from the temple. The unsuspected Essenes in the council urged on his arrest and secured his condemnation. It was arranged that powerful drugs would allow Yeshua to endure the utmost pain and resist death for a long time. Nicodemus made sure that the execution would follow immediately upon the sentence and timed it so that the crucified remained only a short time upon the cross. The centurion had been bribed not to allow any of his bones to be broken. As soon as Yeshua was brought to the grave, the Essenes started a powerful healing process with herbs that would allow him to recover quickly. On Sunday morning, they took him away to a secret place from which he later appeared several times to his disciples...

Venturini's *"A non-supernatural History of the Great Prophet of Nazareth* follows a similar scenario. He differs a bit from Bahrdt about Yeshua's condemnation and execution: It was agreed in full Essene conclave that Yeshua should go up to Jerusalem and publicly proclaim himself as Messiah, then he was to try to disabuse the people of their earthly Messianic expectations, but the plan did not work out. Although the triumphal entry succeeded in having him being hailed as Messiah, when he tried to explain that he was a different kind of Messiah that the one they expected, that severe trials awaited them all, that he showed himself but seldom at the temple instead of taking his place at their head, they began to doubt him. He was suddenly arrested and quickly crucified. His death was not a piece of play-acting; he really expected to die and only meet his disciples again in the eternal life of the other world. But when he so soon gave up the ghost, Joseph of Arimathea had some premonition and requested his body to Pontius Pilate, took him away quickly to the tomb where he was healed. The two "angels" seen by the women were two Essene brethren...

According to the German theologian Heinrich E.G. Paulus, who wrote in 1828, Yeshua's apparent death was actually a trance, the proof being that the loud cry he uttered immediately before his head sank down shows that his strength was very far from being exhausted. The cool grave and the healing herbs made him come back to consciousness. The stone rolled away from the mouth of the grave was an effect of the earthquake. The German theologian Karl A. Hase wrote in 1829 that a stringent proof that Jesus had actually died on the cross cannot be established since there is no evidence that corruption of his body had set in and that is the only infallible sign of death. It is therefore possible that the so-called resurrection was only a return to consciousness after a death-like trance. The sources, however point to a supernatural event. Both the historical possible views – either that the Creator gave new life to a body which was really dead, or that the latent life reawakened in a body which was only seemingly dead – recognize in the resurrection a manifest proof of the care of Providence for the cause of Yeshua, and are therefore both to be recognized as Christian.

Christian H. Weisse, wrote in 1838 that the picture which the *Gospel of Mark* gives of Yeshua is drawn by an imaginative disciple of the faith, filled with the glory of his subject, whose enthusiasm is consequently sometimes stronger than his judgment. For him, the most striking case of the formation of myth is the story of the resurrection. He considered that here too myth must have attached itself to an historical fact. He wrote that the fact in question is not the empty grave, which only came in the story later, when the Jews had spread the report that the body had been stolen from the grave in order to counteract the Christian belief in the resurrection. In consequence of this report, the empty grave had necessarily to be taken up into the story, the Christian account now making use of the fact that the body of Yeshua had not been found as a proof of his bodily resurrection. The emphasis on the identity of the body which was buried with that which rose again, of which the Fourth Evangelist makes so much, belongs to a time when the Church had to oppose the Gnostic conception of a spiritual, incorporeal immortality. The reaction against Gnosticism is, as Weisse rightly remarks, one of the most potent factors in the development of myth in the Gospel history. What then is the historical fact in the resurrection? Only the existence of a personal belief of the apostles and their companions in the miraculous presence of the risen Yeshua in the visions and appearances which they experienced, not the belief of the later Christian Church in the myth of Yeshua's bodily resurrection. Weisse thus combined historical with psychological considerations. For Friedrich W. Ghillany, in 1864, the belief in the resurrection rests upon the visions of the disciples, which are to be explained by their intense desire for the Parousia, of which Jesus had given them the promise...][87]

---

[87] Albert Schweitzer, *The Quest for the historical Jesus*, 1906

Some modern scholars like Michael Baigent in *The Jesus Papers*[88] also claim that Yeshua did not die on the cross; their version has a lot of parallels with Bahrdt and Venturini's stories. Pontius Pilatus – who could not find any fault in Yeshua – condemned him but took steps to ensure he would survive. Yeshua thus spent only three or six hours on the cross, according to the Gospels. When Joseph of Arimathea requested his body, Pilatus was amazed that he had died so quickly (*Mark*), as crucified people would die within one to three days, sometimes even more, some mauled by wild animals. He asked confirmation from the centurion, (who some say was a secret follower of Yeshua, like Nicodemus and Joseph of Arimathea, and later on allegedly became a bishop), who did not pierce his heart with his spear but just strongly poked him on the side to see if he was reacting. His legs were not broken on purpose. Strangely enough, there was no *rigor mortis*. Yeshua was then carefully taken down from the cross, hurriedly carried nearby to Joseph of Arimathea's recently dug out grave; he was laid down on the side of the tomb on a cloth which covered him completely. [This would possibly become the famous antic relic – maybe first known as the Mandalion in Edessa – now called the Turin shroud. It shows precisely specific marks of blood proving that he was still alive as corpses do not bleed, and it has therefore been officially dismissed by the Church as a 14th century fabrication in spite of the clear dating of other analyses.][89] Then he was taken care by Essenes healers, who enveloped him fully with a big poultice of myrrh and aloes, which were brought in huge quantity (70 pounds!), in which they tied him. They knew they had to act fast, as ladies would be coming to anoint the body so, after intensely healing him, they took him out, dressing him in a simple dress, which made Mary Magdalena mistake him for the gardener until he spoke a few words to her. He was then taken away to a secure place where he could fully heal. To survive crucifixion is a rare event indeed, but it is mentioned by the Jewish historian

---

[88] Harper, San Francisco 2006

[89] Holger Kersten, *Jesus lived in India*, Penguin books, London, 1994

Josephus about three men, two of whom died shortly after in spite of being cared for by the best Roman doctors. The other one lived...

The Indian view is also that Yeshua did not die on the cross but entered into a mystic trance which made him look like dead. The greatest exponent of Vedic culture and its essence, *bhakti-yoga*, in the West - A.C. Bhaktivedanta Swami Prabhupada – wrote and spoke, *"Jesus-Christ risked his life for the cause of spreading God consciousness. However, it would be superficial to think that he was ever killed."* (*Bhagavad-gita as it is*, 11.55, Purport.) *"Jesus Christ was being crucified. Still, he was so much compassionate that he prayed saying, 'My father, these rascals do not know what they are doing. So I request You to forgive them.' This is [the nature of a] devotee. Personally, he is suffering, but he is still compassionate. There was an article recently, that Jesus-Christ, although he was crucified, did not die. He went to Kashmir. Some historical references are there. So actually, since he was a representative of God, son of God, how could these rascals kill him? It was a show only... So, when I heard this historical discovery, I was very much pleased, because I was very sorry that Jesus-Christ had been crucified"* (Paris 740615). *"So, the news was there that after crucifixion Jesus-Christ was alive and he went to Kashmir. So, by the yogic process, in samadhi one can remain alive although superficially it is seen that he is killed. That is possible"* (Mauritius 751026). *"Formerly, from Kashmir to Central Asia, it was known as Bhu-svarga, especially Kashmir. Heaven on earth, heaven on the earthly planet."* (Teheran 760807)

So when it is said that Jesus-Christ went to heaven, yes, after being healed, he went to Kashmir, heaven on Earth, Bhu-svarga. Hence there was no resurrection *per se*.

Chapter six
About Miracles

I quote again the opinions of theologians from Dr A. Schweitzer's book. A few German scholars wrote lives of Jesus based on rationalism, beginning with Johann Jakob Hess in 1768, followed by Reimarus in 1774, who wrote that Jesus effected cures but that they were miraculous in the eyes of his contemporaries; that other miracles have no basis in fact but owe their place in the narratives to typology, the attempt to repeat in the case of Jesus but on a grander scale the miracle-stories of the Old Testament. It is quite possible because it does look like Jesus' miracles are copied on Elijah's and Elisha's but surpass them. For instance, Elisha allegedly fed one hundred men with twenty loaves of bread and there were leftovers (4 *Kings* 4:1-44) so Jesus fed five thousand men with five bread-loaves and had twelve extra basketfuls. They allegedly raised children from the dead, so did he.

[For the early German school of rationalism, miracles no longer played a part of any importance. It was a firmly established principle for them that the teachings of Jesus and religion in general hold their place solely in virtue of their inner reasonableness, not by the support of outward evidence. Whenever they could explain a miracle by natural causes, they did not hesitate. Moreover, the problem of the life of Jesus was solved for them the moment they succeeded in bringing Jesus near to their own time, in portraying him as a great teacher of virtue, and in showing that his teachings are identical with the intellectual truth which rationalism deifies. Franz Volkmar Reinhard's work, for instance, published in 1781, leads only to the conclusion that Jesus is to be regarded as a wonderful divine teacher whose plan for the welfare of mankind was incomparably higher than anything which hero or sage had ever striven for. Moral instruction, according to Reinhard, was the principal content and the very essence of Jesus' discourses and his efforts were directed to the establishment of a purely ethical organization. It was important to overthrow superstition and to bring religion in the domain of reason. For Reinhard Jesus was a social reformer, but the point of primary importance was the alliance of religion with reason. Venturini explained away in 1800 the raisings from the dead as cases of coma, and the changing of water in wine at Cana by Yeshua having brought with him as a wedding-gift some jars of good wine which he had put aside in another room. Johann Adolph Jakobi in 1816 wrote that much of the miraculous was a later addition to the facts, but he thought that a certain amount of miracle must be maintained, but not for the purpose of founding belief on it. He wrote that the miracles were not intended to authenticate Jesus' teachings but "to surround his life with a guard of honor". Having a rooted distrust of thoroughgoing rationalism, he said that "its would-be helpful explanations were often stranger than the miracles themselves".

In 1828, Heinrich Eberhard Gottlob Paulus, who had a deep distrust of anything that went outside the boundaries of logical thought, published a work based on fully developed rationalism. He wrote, *"How empty would devotion or religion be if one's spiritual well-being depended on whether one believed in miracles or no! The truly miraculous thing about Jesus is himself, the purity and serene holiness of his character, which is, notwithstanding, genuinely human, and adapted to the imitation and emulation of mankind."* He explained away miracles as consisting merely in the fact that at that time miracles entered into the plan of God, in the sense that the minds of men were to be astounded and subdued by inexplicable facts; so eyewitnesses reported events of which they didn't know the secondary causes, as their knowledge of the laws of nature was insufficient to enable to understand what had actually happened. Sometimes Jesus worked with his spiritual power upon the nervous system of the sufferer; sometimes he used powerful medicines known to him alone; there was no raisings from the dead, but from cataleptic trance or coma, and deliverances from premature burial, which at that time was taking place 3 hours after death in Judaea; the oil the disciples were anointing sick people with were of a medicinal character, and the casting out of evil spirits was effected partly by means of sedatives. Jewish love of miracle caused everything extraordinary to be ascribed immediately to the Deity. Karl A. Hase in 1828 and Friedrich Schleiermacher in 1832 both had also recourse to rationalistic explanations of the miracles attributed to Jesus, but they are described by A. Schweitzer as the "sceptics of rationalism" leaving open the possibility of miracle. Weisse interpreted the miracles in 1838 as facts later embellished with a mythical element.

David Strauss in 1835 applied a mythological explanation to the Gospel, stating that *"myth forms the lofty gateways at the entrance to, and at the exit from, the Gospel history"*. In a Hegelian way, he presented his mythological interpretation as the synthesis of the thesis of the super-naturalistic explanation of the events of Jesus' life and the antithesis of the rationalistic explanation of the same. In other words, he set up the hypothesis that the inexplicable elements in the Gospel are mythical and that the Gospels contain several different strata of legend and narrative sometimes intersecting and at other times superimposed one upon the other, the creative activity of legend confusing the account of what really happened. For instance, he stated that if the resurrection was real then the death was not real, and vice versa. He showed with an admirable dialectic skill the total impossibility of any explanation which does not take account of myth, favoring however the super-naturalistic explanation over the rationalistic. He wrote that, *"No sooner is a great man dead than legend is busy with his life...The essential character of religious myth is that it is nothing else than the clothing in historic form of religious ideas, shaped by the unconsciously inventive power of legend."* He admitted that the eschatological statements which the Evangelists put into Jesus' mouth may have only been an expression of pious hope and that we cannot determine the part which the expectations of primitive Christianity may have had in molding these statements. With Strauss began the period of the non-miraculous view of Jesus' life. Christian Wilke recognized in 1837 in *Tradition and myth* that Strauss had given an exceedingly valuable impulse towards the overcoming of rationalism and supernaturalism and to the rejection of the abortive mediating theology: "*A keener criticism will only establish the truth of the Gospel, putting what is tenable on a firmer basis, sifting out what is untenable...*"He thought that the time had come for a rational mysticism and reproached to Strauss his mythical realism in which philosophy does violence to history and the historic Christ only retains his significance as a mere ideal.

For Christoph von Ammon in 1842, "*The sacred history is subject to the same laws as all other narratives of antiquity so a miraculous event can only exist when its natural causes have been discovered. Only historically conceivable miracles can be admitted. In every natural process, we have to suppose, according to Kant, an interpenetration of natural and supernatural. For that very reason, the supernatural does not exist for our experience...We shall hold it to be our duty to call attention to the natural side even of the miracles of Jesus.*" For him, the terrible fate of Yeshua at the hands of the Jews was due to the fact that "*the mass of their people were not prepared to receive a messiah so spiritual as Jesus was since they were not ripe for so lofty a view of religion.*"

From the historical point of view, it is impossible to solve the problem of miracle since we are not able to reconstruct the process by which a series of miracle stories arose, or a series of historical occurrences were transformed into miracle stories, and these narratives must simply be left with a question mark standing against them. The exclusion of miracle from our view of history has been universally recognized as a principle of historical criticism, so that miracle no longer concerns the historian, either positively or negatively. The foundation laid by Strauss is unshakable. Christian H. Weisse hailed Strauss' *Life of Jesus* as a forward step towards the reconciliation of religion and philosophy. He thought that Christianity could not afford to deprive itself of the aid of the latter.

Ernest Renan refused in 1863 to assert either the possibility or the impossibility of miracle but spoke as an historian, writing that he was not saying that a miracle is impossible but was only saying that there has never been a satisfactorily authenticated miracle. A. Schweitzer's explanation of the feeding of the multitude is that the whole event is historical, except the closing remark that they were all filled. He wrote that the crowd actually only received a very little, but that it was consecrated food, and that meal became without their knowledge a sacrament of salvation, a guarantee of partaking in the coming Messianic feast and being received in the Kingdom of God. He wrote the same about the Last Supper. He compared both to the baptism by John who was guaranteeing the people he baptized with water that they would be later on baptized with the Holy Spirit, and, having been signed with the mark of repentance, would receive forgiveness of their sins at the time of the Judgment.][90]

The British philosopher Hume said about miracles that they could be accepted as facts only if a naturalistic explanation would be even more far-fetched than a supernatural one.

---

[90] *The Quest for the historical Jesus*

Chapter seven
Was Jesus created by the Romans?

Cicero advised to use religion for the good of the state, advocating to persuade the masses to follow the theology most appropriate for it,[91] so religion may also be manipulated or even created for a mundane purpose. Joseph Atwill[92] claims that Jesus' persona was completely created by the Romans, specifically the Flavian family which consisted of three Caesars – Vespasian and his two sons, Titus and Domitian. Roman emperors were already trying to control Judaism for their own interests, micromanaging it by appointing its high priests from a circle of families allied to Rome. They were confronted to the nationalistic, militaristic and messianic Jewish movement of the Sicarii or Zealots, who emerged around 40 BC.[93] Those Sicarii, who were waiting for a military messiah, are mentioned in the Gospels as militantly active during the lifetime of Yeshua. They revolted and finally succeeded in defeating the Romans in 66 CE. But a civil war erupted between the moderates led by former Head Priest Ananos, the Zealots of Eleazar ben Simon, the partisans of John of Gischala, and the group of Simeon bar Giora. The repression of the revolt, led by Vespasian on the order of the emperor Nero, then by Titus, was terrible. The temple of Jerusalem was destroyed in 70 CE and the last stronghold of the Sicarii, Masada, was captured in 73 CE. Although the revolt had been repressed,

---

[91] *The laws* 2:15-16

[92] *Caesar's Messiah*

[93] Hellenism had spread in Judea after Alexander the Great's conquest in 333 BC. Antiochus III of the Seleucid dynasty (which began with Seleceus, a general of Alexander) snatched Judea and southern Syria from the Lagidis in 200BC. Antiochus IV crushed a revolt against the polytheism and rationalism of Hellenism led by the Maccabees in 168 BC, killing 40 000 Jews and enslaving the same amount. But the Maccabees kept on fighting; after 20 years they finally defeated the Seleucids and ruled Israel for around 100 years, creating the Hasmonean dynasty, until the Romans took over in 40BC. The Sicarii then started to rebel.

many Jews continued to believe and hope that their deity would send a warrior messiah to free them. Assisted by two powerful Hellenized Jewish families, the Herods and the Alexanders, with whom they shared the control of the region, the Flavians imagined a device to deprive messianic xenophobic Judaism of its power to spawn revolts.

They claimed that the messiah the Jews were waiting for had actually already come in the person of Yeshua, replacing the militaristic messianic movement by a pacifistic religion that supposedly was favorable to the Empire, willingly accepted Roman rule, taught to turn the other cheek, walk an extra mile when conscripted to carry a Roman soldier's package for one mile, and give to Caesar what was his due (Mark 12:17)[94]. In this way, Yeshua was muzzled. His statement, *"My kingdom is not of this world"* is a probable interpolation by Romans to pretend that Yeshua was not a revolutionary messiah but a spiritual one speaking not of booting the Romans out of Israel but of a heavenly kingdom. *"The Romans created a 'domesticated' messiah. The Messiah Jesus defined in the New Testament was a savior with Roman values, not the values of the militant Judaism found in the scrolls...Christianity was created to be an alternative to the type of rebellious Judaism that swept across Judea in the first century CE...The religion that was the basis of Western morality was invented for the pacification of slaves."*

---

[94] Another explanation of this famous passage is given by Thom Stark in *The Human Faces of God*: *"On the surface, Jesus' answer to the question if it was right to pay taxes to Caesar appears to legitimize taxation to Caesar. But the reality is that Jesus and his audience knew fully well how crippling the Roman taxes and tributes were on the peasant population. Moreover, inscribed on the Roman coin held up by Jesus was a claim of divine sonship for the Roman emperor. Every self-respecting Jew would know the meaning and subject of Jesus' response. The audience knew how to parse out Jesus' aphorism. What rightfully belongs to Caesar? Nothing. What rightfully belongs to God? Everything...But if Jesus was alluding to a hidden transcription of opposition to Rome while answering that question, it's not how his words have been read through much church history. If Jesus' language was a subversion of the official transcript, the reality is that his language has only been subject to counter-subversion by the ruling elites ever since. Mark 12:17 has been used by governments to impose the most oppressive of taxes upon populations for centuries."*

Yeshua allegedly taught the holiness of subservience to one's master or ruler. He is quoted saying that he had not found such a great faith as a Roman Centurion's in the whole of Israel (*Luke* 7:1-9). Another Centurion, Cornelius is described as a devout, God-fearing man, always praying God (*Acts* 10:1-2). Apostle Matthew was a publican, a tax-collector for the Romans. Pilatus, the Roman consulate is said to "wash his hands from the fate of this just man." That episode, indeed, seems suspect. Paul's epistle states that rebelling against one's ruler is revolting against God, who has made him a ruler for your benefit (*Rom*.13:2-6). How could this be? How historically illogical! How could such a movement emerge from a nation bitterly struggling against Rome? How could Yeshua, the supposed Jewish Messiah, have had such a diametrically different political perspective than the scion of David expected by all the Jews, who *"would have garments dipped in blood, would kill kings and rulers and redden the mountains with their blood"*[95]? How did an originally oral Aramaic tradition end up being written in literary Greek by illiterate apostles? How is it that early Christianity had a Roman worldview, envisioning itself to conquer the world and become its only religion? Why does the Church authority structure resemble the Roman military? Why among all cities was Rome, the capital of the hated Roman conquerors, chosen to be the Church's headquarters and its bishop made the supreme pontiff? A Roman origin would explain how a Judean cult became the state religion and why so many members of the imperial family, the Flavians, are recorded among the first Roman Christians. Indeed, one of the fist popes was Clement I (35-66 CE), son of consul Titus Flavius Sabinus! After Simon Peter ordained him, thus handing the control of the messianic movement to the Flavian family, he was later allegedly martyrized by Emperor Domitian, a member of the same family, whose sister Domitilla founded the first Christian catacomb in Rome!

The Romans were quite tolerant of other religions; they did not fight against the various gods worshipped in their different

---

[95] The *Targum* (the Aramaic version of the Torah)

provinces but absorbed them, harnessing their powers to maintain Pax Romana, which they called *Pax Deorum*, the "peace of the gods". They even elaborated a ritual, the *devotio*, to induce their adversaries' gods to defect to their own camp, thus neutralizing their divine assistance. One Roman soldier would solemnly devote the enemies' troops and himself to the Roman gods and the enemies' deity, then charge, sacrificing his life for the good of the many in exchange for the gods' assistance in taking the enemy down. In the case of Yeshua, the high priest Caiaphas expressed the belief that he, one man, should die for the Jewish people: he should be sacrificed so that the Romans do not destroy the whole nation. (*John* 11: 49-51) Later, self-appointed apostle Paul would take that idea to a completely different dimension, giving it an altogether different meaning. For the Flavians, Yeshua's sacrifice was very much like a *devotio*. They hoped that the religion they established would considerably help to neutralize the militaristic messianic movement of the Sicarii, not just saving Roman troops but the whole Roman world. The German scholar Bruno Bauer also believed that Christianity was Rome's attempt to create a religion that encouraged slaves to accept their fate.

Flavius Josephus – a native of Judea, born in 37 CE and a contemporary of the Apostles – was previously a Jewish revolutionary, Josephus bar Matthias, who was captured; he presented himself as a prophet to general Vespasian and declared that God had revealed to him that He was switching His favor from the Jews to the Romans and that the Jewish messianic prophecies did not specify that the messiah would be a Jew but would be…Vespasian himself. When the Roman general became emperor, he adopted Josephus and gave him his own family name, Flavius. Josephus became their official historian and they "created" the personage of Jesus, according to J. Atwill. They edited the New Testament to replace the literature of Judaism, demonstrating that Christianity was the fulfillment of its prophecies, while satirically lampooning Yeshua and many characters, like those of the Sicarii rebel leaders Simon bar Giora and John of Gischala as Yeshua's disciples Simon and John. (For instance, both Simons were leaders of a Jewish messianic movement who died as martyrs in Rome the same year!) The Romans could not relate to Judaism, which due to its monotheism denying the reality of other peoples' gods, had a strong sense of religious separatism, which made absorption of Judaism into the Roman empire impossible and was one of the causes of its conflict with Rome. For instance, only circumcised Jews could eat the Passover lamb. The New Testament ended that separatism by creating a human Passover lamb in the person of Yeshua, who told his disciples to symbolically eat his flesh and drink his blood.

The Romans attacked Jerusalem precisely at the time of the Jewish Passover celebration, when the festival had gathered many people; so it is quite a cruel satire if it is the Romans who invented the idea of a human Passover lamb, because the famished besieged Jews resorted to cannibalism![96]Flavius Josephus wrote about a Jewish mother called Mary killing and eating her own child during the famine which occurred during that siege, telling her child, *"Be my food and become a fury to the rebels against Rome, and a myth to the world which will complete the calamities of us, Jews."* There were no witnesses to that speech, so Josephus must have invented it. The incoherent phrase becomes intelligible if it is read as a lampoon of Yeshua: The spreading of the myth of a Yeshua killed by the Jews will complete their destruction. Thus the Romans created Christianity to be a calamity upon the Jews. Moreover, by claiming that it was the Jews who were responsible for Yeshua's death, the Flavians poisoned their future by creating antisemitism as a vengeance. Flavius Josephus is known as an historian, but he was specifically the historian of the Flavian emperors. He wrote *Antiquities of the Jews*, *Wars of the Jews*, as well as an autobiography, *The life of Flavius Josephus*. Besides the New Testament, he is the only source of information about this period. None of the chronology of the first century existed until he created it; without him the dating of the events of that time

---

[96] as recorded by Severus, a Roman historian writing in the third century

would not be possible.[97] He was literally creating history and time, so he was free to place events in relation to each other as he chose.

The prophet Daniel's prophecies are so vague that they defy temporal specificity and his visions cover 490 years. Josephus apparently falsified the dates of the events he described in *Wars of the Jews*, placing them in precise time spans relative to one another to create the impression that they were part of Daniel's prophecies, that those came to pass during the 66-73 CE Jewish war and that Yeshua was the Messiah envisioned by Daniel. He was only interested in using history to fulfill his own purpose. His book is entirely structured to document that Daniel's prophecies were coming to pass. For him to remain consistent with his placing events in the context of those prophecies, he placed a messiah at the point in history they called for. The early Christian scholars like Tertullian and Eusebius completely adopted his perspective and his concocted history; they believed that Daniel's prophecies had come to pass in 70 CE. Why did Josephus state so in such a direct manner? Because he knew that the messianic rebels interpreted Daniel's prophecies to try to understand when the Messiah would appear and to justify their militaristic theology.

But why did Josephus take so little notice of Yeshua? Well, it made the forgery less obvious. In order to "create" prophet Yeshua and use him to his own ends, he invented that he existed in the past, then he fabricated a work in his name dated from the time he claimed he lived. In that book, he described Yeshua predicting events that he knew had already occurred. To avoid having the forgery discovered, he made his two fabrications – *Wars of the Jews* and the New Testament – be seen as independent from one another, although they are completely entwined and mutually supportive, and he focused on the events predicted by Daniel and not on the "son of God" himself.

---

[97] The importance of these works to Christians during the Middle Ages was such that Syrian and Armenian hand-written Bibles included them. Later on, with the invention of the printing press, Latin editions of the Bible also included *Antiquities* and *Wars of the Jews*.

Josephus greatly assisted the Romans in their war against the Jews, allegedly convinced that, "*it was God who had brought the Romans to punish the Galileans*" (*Wars of the Jews* 3:7, 291-193), a conviction which grew and became the basis of Christian antisemitism.

Reading those books along the Gospel shows an exact parallel, including the same locations and the same sequence of events, between episodes of Yeshua's preaching campaign and the Roman emperor Titus Flavius' campaign to control the rebellion in Judea. It is clearly a satire. For example, Yeshua told two fishermen on the shore of the lake of Gennesareth that he will make them fishers of men (*Matt.*4:17-19) and Flavius Josephus wrote about a sea battle on the same lake where the Romans literally caught Jewish rebels like fish; they were led by a Jesus (*Wars of the Jews*, 3,10,467). Yeshua exorcized in Gadara a man possessed by a legion of 2000 unclean spirits or demons, who then begged him to send them into a nearby herd of swine; those swine then ran towards the sea, fell into it from a cliff and drowned (*Mark*, 5: 1-20). Flavius Josephus wrote in parallel about the Zealot tyrant John being driven from the same city of Gadara with his men; he conscripted a group of young men in another town and the combined group "running like the wildest of beasts" were slain by the Romans, tried to escape and jumped into the river Jordan where they drowned by the thousands with 2000 of them taken captives (*Wars of the Jews,* 4,7). In *Matthew* 23, Yeshua is wooing eight times the city, the temple, the priests, etc. In *Wars of the Jews* 6.5, Josephus has a Jesus ben Ananias character doing the same for seven years, starting four years before the temple destruction, "*...A voice against Jerusalem and the holy house and against this whole people...*" He was then severely beaten by eminent citizens and, as he kept on uttering the same words as if moved "*by a sort of divine fury*", taken to the Roman procurator "*where he was whipped until his bones were laid bare*", but he kept on crying, "*Woe, woe to Jerusalem!*" He did not answer when he was interrogated by the procurator, who then dismissed him as if he was a madman. During the siege of Jerusalem, as he was again wooing the city, the people and the temple, a stone thrown by a war engine smote him and killed him. That woe-saying Jesus shared the same words, phrases, ideas, experiences and descriptions of the disasters which would come upon Jerusalem and its people with the return of a "Son of Man" than the New Testament Yeshua; the latter, black irony, compared himself to a stone, who, rejected by the builders, becomes the cornerstone which *"will utterly crush one on whom it falls"* (*Matt.*21:42-44).

In his autobiography, as mentioned earlier, Flavius Joseph wrote that while on a mission for Titus Caesar, *"he saw many captives crucified and remembered three of them as his former acquaintances and begged Titus on their behalf, crying. Titus immediately commanded them to be taken down and to have the greatest care of them; yet two of them died in spite of the physician's efforts while the third recovered."* (75, 417, 420-421) The parallel with Yeshua's crucifixion along with two men, and another Josephus, of Arimathea, begging Pilatus to take Yeshua down from the cross is striking. Obviously the writings of Flavius Josephus and the New Testament are connected. One was created with the other in mind. The two documents have too many parallels and exact similarities to have been caused by chance. They were designed to be read intertextually, a traditional Jewish way to read. There were earlier versions of the New Testament, whether oral or written, but at one point the Gospels were rewritten and unified in a satiric whole, aligning them with *Wars of the Jews.* Using typology, the Roman editors of the Gospels created the impression that events from previous prophets were repeated in Yeshua's life, especially Moses', in the very same order: both their births caused distress to a ruler and were followed by a massacre of children, a miraculous rescue and Egypt as the land of that rescue. Moses was chosen as the prototype for Yeshua because he was the founder of the old religion Yeshua was replacing with the new one he was allegedly founding. All four Gospels as well as Paul's Epistles show that Passover and Judaism itself are obsolete, being replaced by Yeshua, the new Passover lamb, and Christianity. Yeshua is quoted as saying that, *"Your fathers ate the manna and died, I am the living bread coming from heaven and whoever eats of it will not die but live forever"* (*John* 6:49-52), to show that it was an improved covenant with God, one who brought life.

Josephus Flavius described in detail the events of that 66-73 CE Jewish war, then retrospective "prophecies" about them were put in Yeshua's mouth in the Gospels, "proving" to the Christians that Yeshua must have been divine to "foresee" them. In other words, what Yeshua had "prophesied", Josephus recorded as having happened. The black irony is that the visitation within the present "wicked generation"(*Matt.*12:39,45) by "the Son of Man" – a title used by prophet Daniel for the Messiah – which Yeshua "foresaw" and "warned" about because it would bring specific disastrous events during it (*Matt.*24:34), was not his return or Second Coming as misunderstood, but the coming of Titus with his troops![98] Only Titus, and not Yeshua, can be said to have fulfilled these "prophecies" about "the Son of Man", such as encircling Jerusalem with a wall and destroying the temple to the last stone. So, was Titus the "Son of Man" prophesized by Yeshua?

Atwill suggests that Titus wanted the Jews to bow down to him as the god he was portrayed to be as the Roman emperor, but since they refused even under torture, he commanded Josephus to write his stories and edit the Gospels so that "the Son of Man" expected by the Jewish Christians and worshipped by them was him, Titus, in reality. *"The real intent of Christianity was to convert the followers of the Jewish messiah into followers of Caesar without their knowing it."* The Gospel establishes Yeshua as Titus' forerunner. That would make Yeshua, whose Second Coming was "prophesized" to happen within that generation (*Matt.*23:6), come back as...Titus??!! The 17th century theologian Reland and his contemporary, William Whiston, understood that Yeshua's "prophecies" indicated that he would come at the head of the Roman army for the destruction of the Jews! So, was Titus the reincarnation of Yeshua appearing to chastise the Jews to have persecuted him and his followers?! *"All the dialogues that describe Jesus' relationship with the Father use comic wordplay*

---

[98] *Caesar's messiah*, Flavian signature edition, 2011 USA

that actually describes Titus' relationship with his father, the emperor and god Vespasian." Seen under that angle, they make perfect sense and flow without contradiction into the cult of the deified emperor.

The name 'Jesus' or Yeshua in Hebrew means savior. The word 'Christ' is Greek for "messiah", the "anointed one". 'Jesus-Christ' or 'Savior Messiah' is not just a name but a title. Anyone seeing himself as sent by God to save Judea could have claimed it. So what was Yeshua's real name? Eusebius (c 260-340 AD) suggests that the name 'Yeshua' may have been allegorical and that he may have been called Yeshua after it became clear that he was the savior. Was more than one person called "Yeshua" or "Christ" in the New Testament? There were many called Eleazar. One messiah Titus fought was called Eleazar ben Simon (allegedly satirized as Lazarus in the Gospel). Atwill suggests that the Romans stole his identity, like Simon's and John's and made him into the historical Christ also said to have been captured on the Mount of Olives. Like attributed to Yeshua, he was born in Galilea, had the power to expel demons, was plotted against by high priests, was scourged and…survived a crucifixion!

The Sicarii regrouped anyway, and later, in 132, launched another attempt to free their land from the Roman occupation. They were led by Simon bar Kosiba, who was also considered a messiah by the Jews. But this revolt, like the previous ones led by the Maccabees, by the Sicarii, by about 50 other people before Jesus – like Jude bar Ezekias, Theudas and Menander, two Samaritans, Judas of Gamala the Galilean (*Acts* 536-37), Jesus ben Hananiah the Egyptian (*Acts* 21:38) etc. – was repressed even more terribly. Josephus writes that another Eleazar convinced the Sicarii defenders of Masada to commit suicide rather than risk being captured. This mass suicide is possibly a fictitious story, a propaganda having the aim of encouraging the rebels to suicide instead of fighting down to the last man and costing the Romans more troops. And Josephus is taking great care to claim that, as with the crucifixion of Yeshua and the destruction of the temple, it is the Jews, not the Romans who are responsible for the slaughter. History is always written by the victors…Joseph Atwill's thesis is bold, provocative and profoundly challenging. As professor Robert Eisenman wrote, *"If what he says is only partially true, we are looking into the abyss."* Could it be possible that the intended target of the Gospels were new Jewish converts or Jews tempted to join the ranks of the messianic militant Zealots, in order to disarticulate the Jewish political and military leverage? Others say that the Romans did not completely create Christianity as a mass religion to counteract the Zealots, stamp out their revolutionary spirit and manipulate slaves into acceptance of their fate, but that they did completely transform Yeshua's message by thoroughly editing the Gospel, turning this revolutionary character into an almost pro-Roman, peaceful religious teacher. From a revolutionary tiger, he was turned into a harmless kitten mewing *"Ave Caesar!"* The entire arsenal of Roman values is embedded within the Christian scriptures; that may have well served to dupe a target population. A religious movement that opposed the Romans militarily was cleverly removed by them from history and replaced with one aligned with their interests, appearing to be God's replacement for Judaism, with Yeshua as the Passover lamb of the "new Judaism". Others suggest that it is not the Romans but later Christians who "sanitized" the Gospel by taking away all or most revolutionary elements from J Yeshua's life and teachings to make it acceptable to the Roman audience and authorities. When read from that perspective, beneath the golden patina of Yeshua's ministry, filled with miracles and pastoral scenes of captivated audiences, there seems to be deep and intentional malice to demonize the Jews and God's covenant with Israel. The early church fathers stated that the righteous characters in the Bible were proto-Christians, not Jews: *"from Abraham himself to the first man [Adam], they were Christians in fact if not in name"*[99]. Muhammad, the prophet of Islam, will claim later that those Biblical characters were not Jews nor Christians but Muslims!

---

[99] Eusebius, *Ecclesiastical History* I, iv

The twin theory

'Thomas' means 'twin' in Greek. In *The Bible Fraud*, Tony Bushby writes that Jesus had a twin brother, Judas Thomas, who was also the leader of a group of followers. *"The earliest oral and written traditions relay a confused skeletal outline of the lives of two separate men – these two brothers – which have been amalgamated in time into one."* Indeed, the Gnostic Christians believed Judas Thomas was the twin brother of Yeshua. That Jesus had a twin was debated for centuries. Michelangelo and Leonardo da Vinci both portrayed twin sons of Mary. The Essenes believed in a New Covenant and the coming of two messiahs, one priestly, the other military. Those mystic schools and communities (Essenes, Therapeuts, Hermetics, Gnostics, etc.) which were later on called "heretics" by the orthodoxy are inextricably interwoven with nascent Christianity. The idea that Jesus had a twin, Judas, who obviously could not have the same character and demeanor, could explain the paradoxical behavior attributed to Jesus – like his saying that he was a drunkard and glutton (*Luke* 7:34, *Matthew* 11:19); his saying that he had not come to bring peace but division (*Luke* 12:51, *Matt.*10:35-36); his commanding to hate one's family members (*Luke* 14:26); his cursing a fig tree for not supplying figs whereas it was out of season (*Mark* 11:12-20); his driving out the money-changers in the temple with a whip of cords, overturning the tables and seats (*John* 2:15); his being referred to as possessed by a demon or mad in six places in the Gospel; his not washing before dinner and blasting with a full-scale verbal assault the Pharisee who commented upon it (*Luke* 11:38); his telling his followers to sell their coat and buy a sword if they didn't have one, etc. According to Bushby, this was not Jesus' doing but Judas Thomas'. His followers were mostly Galileans, a term synonymous with aggressive militant and war-mongering anti-Roman nationalists. They were his militia, distinct from the apostles, the disciples of His twin, Rabbi Yeshua/Jesus, who had a different behavior altogether. In a manuscript, *The Lives of the Caesars*, published about 120AD attributed to Suetonius (69-140CE) it is mentioned that Emperor Claudius expelled all Jews from Rome because of disturbances instigated there by the followers of a man called Khrestus, an expulsion confirmed in *Acts* (18:2-3). In a manuscript which surfaced in 1427, Tacitus (55-120CE), a classical Roman historian, is also mentioning in his Annals a man called Khrestus or Christus who was crucified at the hands of Pontius Pilate during the reign of Tiberius. *"Nero fastened the guilt and inflicted the most exquisite tortures on a class hated for their abominations, called Christians by the populace. Christus, from whom the name had its origin, suffered the extreme penalty during the reign of Tiberius at the hands of one of our procurators, Pontius Pilatus, and a most mischievous superstition, thus checked for the moment, again broke out not only in Judæa, the first source of the evil, but even in Rome"* (*Annals* 15.44). Christians usually say this refers to Jesus, but Tony Bushby, the author of *The Bible Fraud*, suggests it was Judas Thomas, Jesus' twin.

It is important to remain mindful that New Testament scholarship is highly speculative and based on making and testing hypotheses. Indeed, in dealing with the Gospel traditions, who can realistically offer proof positive of any thesis? By wanting at all cost to find connections between inexplicable passages in the narrative of *Mark* which, if analyzed more deeply, do not fit together although they are found next to each other, and by wanting to find an answer to many questions raised by such thorough analysis, scholar and layman alike import various elaborate psychological analyses into texts where nothing of the sort is found at all. They see what they believe, giving credence to interpretations and information they support while dismissing that which they oppose. Their interpretations are detached from their context and transform everything. They retain the portion of the traditional sayings of Yeshua which can fit in their particular idea of what possibly happened – the kernel of history, as they label it arbitrarily – and dismiss as spurious or interpolated whatever does not fit into their scenario. They read in those texts and assert as self-evident things that are not even hinted at by the Evangelists. A. Schweitzer wrote in conclusion to his book that,

"Historical criticism was concerned for the religious interests of the present and its rationalistic bias had made it become a secret

struggle to reconcile the Germanic religious spirit with the Spirit of Jesus of Nazareth, projecting back into history what belonged to its own time, wanting to bring their "historical Jesus" into the midst of their time... We modern theologians are too proud of our historical method, of our historical Jesus, too confident in our belief in the spiritual gains which our historical knowledge can bring to the world. We have weakened down his great imperious sayings, his imperative world-condemning demands upon individuals, so that he might not come into conflict with our ethical ideals and might tune his denial of the world to our acceptance of it. It is nothing less than misfortune for modern theology that it mixes history with everything and ends by being proud of the skill with which it finds its own thought in Jesus and represents him as expressing them. The abiding eternal in Jesus is absolutely independent of historical knowledge and can only be understood by contact with his spirit. In proportion as we have the Spirit of Jesus, we have the true knowledge of Jesus."

Chapter eight
Saving the Christians

What is Christianity based upon?

As suggested in the introduction, it should be more adequately called "Pauline Christianity" as it rests mainly if not solely on Paul's four first concoctions:

1. Adam and Eve were created perfect and immortal.

2. they sinned by eating the fruit of a tree.

3. the salary of sin is death.

4. their Original Sin was and is transmitted to all human beings.

Then come his other four inventions:

1. Jesus-Christ willingly chose to give his life as a vicarious atonement for all people' sins.

2. He was the long-expected Jewish messiah.

3. He is God's special and only son.

4. He is non-different from God.

These eight claims have actually no other basis than Paul's imagination. Faith is only as good as what you believe in. As explained in Lee Strobel's book *The real case for Jesus*, faith must be based on indisputable evidence; there must be a confirmation of the authenticity of the facts one believes in by a recognized authority, whose credibility is beyond any suspicion. Why don't the Christian apologists apply to Paul's ideas the rigor they say should be applied, like: *"Who wrote the document? When was it written? Does it reflect the culture of the time? Was this person in a position to know what happened? Was he motivated by prejudice or bias?"* We saw earlier that Paul invented four things not confirmed at all by the Old Testament of the Bible. No Jewish religious authority confirmed any of them. So what is the value of his statements? What is the basis of his authority? And where is the solid evidence backing up his four next claims? There is not the least key piece of evidence for any of them. And again no Jewish authority confirmed them, quite the contrary. There are only his words in his epistles to new converts, nothing else. And that too is questionable as we saw earlier. He was undoubtedly a great, indefatigable, dedicated preacher. But a preacher of what? Of which truths? He stayed away from the original disciples of Yeshua and preached his own ideas. They did not confirm any of them, and Yeshua did not express any of them either.

Paul turned Yeshua into the persona of "Christ", born from his fertile brain. He or his followers later on, according to many scholars, divinized that "Christ", claiming that God is invisible but became visible in his form, *"Jesus-Christ is the visible image of the invisible God"* (*Col*.1:15). He also stated that, *"By him everything was created. In him all the fullness of God was dwelling"* (*Col*.1:16, 19). However, Yeshua never made any claim of divinity. In fact, there are places where he suggests the contrary: *"Why do you call me good? No one is good but God alone* (*Mark* 10:18; *Luke* 18:19). He never claimed to be God and always referred to his "Father", whom he said was greater than himself, like in *John* 6:38,14:28, 16:28 or in *Revelation* 3:12 where he says, *"my God"*. He never claimed either that he was the *Logos*, the Word of God, who created everything. God is the sole creator. This conception is a later concoction of the author of *John* who drew for the formulation of his own theology from the writings of Philo of Alexandria (20BC-c50AD) who, in a Jewish Hellenistic syncretism, attempted to marry Hellenism and the Torah by combining Plato and Moses into a single philosophical system, a new wisdom which Christianity was believed to bring to completion. Philo had developed a concept of the *Logos* as God's creative principle.

Not only did Paul say that Jesus-Christ was God; he also said, "*He died on the cross to wash all sins by his blood*" (*Col*.1.20). However, Yeshua never said that he would willingly die for everyone's sins and none of his direct followers believed that; they did not follow him out of the hope that they would be saved from their sins when he would offer himself for sacrifice. One of them even tried to defend him when the soldiers came to arrest him![100] If you think about it, the belief that he died for people's sins and received the punishment that they deserved is completely unethical at its root. It would be as if, in a court of law, a murderer sentenced to death would find another person who was willing to die in his place, and the murderer would then be set free. However, even if one believes that Jesus-Christ died to atone for one's sins, freedom from sin is not the only qualification to enter God's spiritual world of love. As Yeshua is quoted to have said in the Parable of the Wedding Feast,[101] one needs a special dress to attend the wedding; that is the dress of pure love, not just freedom from sin. One cannot enter the spiritual kingdom of God without having developed pure love for Him... And social action is not an act of love towards God. It is based on a misunderstanding of Yeshua's words that whatever one does to "the smallest of mine" one is doing to him, where he meant by that something done to his disciples not to just any human being.

Paul interpreted some of Yeshua's parables, like the one of the wicked vineyard tenants, to say that Jesus-Christ was God's beloved son. Alright, let us say for the sake of argument that he is, but why claim he is the only son? Yeshua never claimed he was any special son of God, but referred to himself as "the Son of man". That expression in Aramean, as we saw, simply means man or human being. It does not imply a divine status but rather a

---

[100] Matt. 26:51-2

[101] *Matthew* 22.1-14

prophetical status, as used in the book of Daniel. Yeshua never claimed either to be the "only son of God", but that we are all God's children. He taught his followers to pray, *"Pater Noster... Our Father who is in heavens..."*

What are the Paulinian Christians taught to believe?

There is quite a peculiar creed in Pauline Christianity: God decided, *"I am going to create man and woman perfect and immortal but nonetheless sinful by nature!? They will sin and lose their immortal status and that first sin will have to be shared by all their descendants. Then I am going to mystically impregnate a woman with My only son – who is non-different from Myself – as her child in order to take birth on Earth, but she will remain a virgin. Then I am going to sacrifice Myself – under the form of My son – unto Myself, to save my foolish human creatures from the sins born from the nature I created them with!"* This creed is a series of blatant contradictions and can only be accepted on the basis of blind faith. Anyone who stops to think and analyze it cannot help but distinguish its fallacies: If someone is perfect, he cannot be sinful! If someone is immortal, which means he will never die, he cannot stop being immortal! Sin is individual not shared! God is unlimited, so why ascribe to Him a one and only son? Man and God belong to two different ontological categories and God's body, although looking like a man's body, is immaterial! How can a woman give birth and remain a virgin through the process? God does not share man's fallen condition and never dies! It is indeed a strange vision of a world where God feels that He must kill His own son because He can find no other way to forgive people for the sins they commit due to the nature they have been created with?! Does an omnipotent Creator need to send a redeemer, and in such a cruel way?

Why would God require a blood sacrifice to forgive people of their sins? It seems to be born from the old Semitic idea that a human sacrifice could appease the sanguinary deities. The concept that Jesus-Christ had to be crucified as a kind of scapegoat in order for God to forgive people' sins is absurd. *"A human father who would nail his son to a cross for any purpose would be arrested for child-abuse.*"[102] God could just as easily have forgiven sins based on prayers or simply having earnest regret. The Bible says that God alone is the True Deity, the only Savior and that He alone can forgive sin (*Isaiah* 43:10, 11, 25). Shri Krishna says the same at the end of the *Bhagavad-gita*, "*Give up all your mundane duties and various religious processes. Just surrender unto Me. I will free you from all the results of your sins. I will protect you. Do not hesitate, do not fear*" (18-65)

The Bible clearly states that everyone pays for his own sins. People should not kid themselves and be so gullible to think that all their sins have been forgiven just because they believe that someone (Yeshua/Jesus-Christ) died for them, instead of themselves paying for their own sins. To want something to be true does not make it true, no matter how strongly you want it and believe it. This Paulinian myth of Yeshua/Jesus-Christ an hybrid God-man absorbing sin and dying for them is totally illogical. God does not die! God does not become a human being subjected to death! By his speculation about God sending His "only" son – as if God could not have more than one and is thus less than His creatures – to die on the cross for the sins of all men, Paul created the idea of a terrible God. "*It was the Christian tradition that produced atheism as its fruit; it led to the murder of God in the conscience of men because it presented them with an unbelievable God.*"[103]

To believe that someone has taken the load of your sins on himself instead of you carrying it may be a wonderful relief from the fear coming along with that burden, but it has very grave consequences. This could easily be blind, unfounded faith and wishful thinking. One may be in for a surprise when he leaves his body, thinking he is going to heaven, or at worst to Purgatory (another non-Biblical invention) whereas he may find himself in one of the hellish planets to pay for his sins and then reincarnate

---

[102] Episcopal Bishop John Shelby Spong. *Why Christianity must change or die.* Harper, San Francisco, 1999

[103] P. Valadier

again like everyone else who has not developed pure love of God. You cannot "believe away" your sins. Magic plays absolutely no role in the system of sin and atonement established by God. Atonement by "faith" is not part of God's setup. But Paul insisted that Yeshua/Jesus-Christ made a New Covenant, which cancelled the supposed old Abrahamic one, and that one was not anymore subjected to the Mosaic law but was under the grace of God Jesus. He reversed the Jewish theology by viewing Yeshua/Christ as a God-man and viewing his death as a final sacrifice for the propitiation of sins, making unnecessary any further animal sacrifices that were standard rituals in the Jewish temples. Countless millions of people have thus been completely misled by Paul's sheer fabrications that Yeshua was God incarnate and that he died voluntarily on the cross like a criminal for everyone's sins. Such a tale was widely transmitted, and many innocent and naive believers gave their lives as martyrs for it.

In contrast, in the *Bhagavad-gita*, Shri Krishna declares that even if someone surrendered to Him commits accidentally or out of past bad habit a very sinful activity, if he repents sincerely, he should still be considered saintly and will quickly become righteous. (*Bgita* 9.30) In the *Brahma-samhita,* Brahma states that there is no place one can hide in the whole universe to escape one's *karma*, except if one does what God wants him to do, which is to dedicate oneself to serve Him with love (*karmani-nindanti kintu ca bhakti-bhajam*). Then all the different stages of sin or *karma* (seed, seedling, immature and mature) as well as ignorance, the very root of *karma*, are gradually uprooted.

There was no Pharisee opposition to Jesus.

There were many Jewish sects in Jesus' times: Pharisees, Sadducees, Sicarii or Zealots, Essenes, plus the estranged Samaritans. In spite of nearly two thousand years of anti-Semitic Christian propaganda – which is clearly visible in the Gospels, whose writers who are supposedly Jews always speak of "the Jews" with animosity as belonging to a different group – the Jews in general, and the Pharisees in particular, did not oppose Yeshua nor his followers, as all were yearning for a messiah who would at last free them from oppression and fulfill the messianic prophecies. They were sympathetic to anyone feeding such hope. A group of Pharisees even came to warn Yeshua to leave Galilea because king Herod was out to kill him (*Luke* 13:31), an advice they could not have given to him, nor could they have expected him to accept, if they were his alleged deadly enemies. According to *Matthew*, Yeshua recognized the legitimacy of their leadership and teachings, telling his disciples, "*Do whatever they teach you and follow it*" while having reservations about them, as he considered them theoretical teachers: "*but don't do as they do for they don't practice what they teach.*"[104]

Hyam Maccoby explains clearly that there was no disagreement between Yeshua and the Pharisees; it is only a later editing of the Gospels which makes it appear that there was. He gives the typical example of the way a respectful amicable conversation between a Pharisee and Jesus in the earliest gospel, *Mark* 12:28-34, is turned into a hostile confrontation in *Matthew* (22:34-40). He underlines the fact that Yeshua's answer that the first commandment is to love God and the second, one's next, are not an original idea of his own but an established part of Pharisee thinking; also that Yeshua's mentioning the "Kingdom of God" was part of Pharisaic phraseology, not a phrase coined by him. Yeshua's famous "revolutionary, epoch-making" statement that the Sabbath was made for man and not man for the Sabbath is found almost word for word in a Pharisee source. His style of preaching through parables is typically Pharisee, and his expression such as a camel going through the eye of a needle belongs to the Pharisee tradition.

Maccoby stresses that the word 'Pharisee' must have been substituted to the original word 'Sadducees' in the other stories where the Pharisees are described as wishing to kill Yeshua for preaching... Pharisee doctrine! He is described as arguing a Pharisee viewpoint about the Sabbath against...Pharisees, which is nonsense! Granted, he was sometimes disagreeing with them and even called them hypocrites because he felt that they were

---

[104] Mat. 23 : 2-3

too much attached to uphold the letter of the law, the subtleties of which they were endlessly arguing about in the typical Jewish *midrash* tradition, and not keen enough to apply the essence of the law – love of God – in their own life. Or to use the oral law to escape their obligations. But his and their teachings concurred. Only the Sadducees, who were the ruling priestly class administrating the Jerusalem Temple and collaborating with the Romans, did oppose Yeshua; as they had more to lose than anyone else, they denounced him to the Romans as a political agitator guilty of treason against Rome for claiming to be the Messiah or king of the Jews. This is actually the basis on which he was judged and crucified. Crucifixion was a punishment inflicted on political grounds, not religious ones. The Romans and not the Jews had the custom to place on the cross of crucifixion the reason for execution. This was done for Yeshua. He may have accepted the title of Messiah, which was an integrant part of Jewish culture. This was a political statement and that got him killed. If the Pharisees were his bitter enemies, why didn't they bring any charges against him at his trial? And if they were friendly to him, why didn't they defend him? The fact is that they were not even present because it was not the Sanhedrin which judged him as we have been led to believe, but a state synedrion, a political tribunal of the High Priest's henchmen which the former presided over. Yeshua's claim to be the Messiah was not blasphemous for the Pharisees and it did not constitute an offence in Jewish law.

At that time, the term 'messiah' was not yet loaded with the meaning of divinity it took later on due to Paul's imagination. So one should not attribute to Yeshua a later concept of his own Messiahship that he did not have and which would have been seen as a blasphemy. Since 'messiah' at that time meant king, the Sadducees accused him of sedition against Rome, but the Gospel editors successfully tried to depict them as having framed and condemned him for a false charge and of accusing him of religious blasphemy rather than political rebellion. The Romans are thus depicted as innocent, having been bamboozled and tricked into condemning him. Pontius Pilate is described as washing his hands of the blame and the Jews as accepting and saying, "*His blood be on us and our children*",[105] a terrible phrase pregnant with many centuries of persecution. Thus the guilt was fully transferred to the Jews. *They* were framed by the Gospel writers, as remarked by Maccoby.

Besides the Sadducees, the Jews in general, and the Pharisees in particular, did not have anything against Yeshua, nor against his original Jewish followers, who were practicing the same orthodox Jewish religion. For instance, Acts – for whatever its historical value is worth – states that when the Sadducees members of the Sanhedrin wanted to condemn apostle Peter to death for his preaching, Gamaliel, a very eminent Pharisee, did not condemn him as a heretic but regarded him as a member of a messianic movement directed against Rome, as some previous ones which he quoted. He took his defense and convinced the council to desist, wait and see, saying that, "*If this sect is from man, it will die out, but if it is from God then you won't be able to stop it and you are running the risk to fight against God*" (Acts 5: 33-39). The only difference of Yeshua's followers with their co-religionists was that they considered him as the long-awaited Messiah. Acts describes them as "*having the goodwill of all the people, and keeping up their daily attendance to the Jerusalem temple*" (2:43-47). And according to Eusebius writing in the 3rd century, the first ten leaders of the Yeshua Jerusalem movement were all circumcised Jews who were keeping the Jewish dietary laws and observing the Sabbath and festivals, which proves that they did not change their religion. That included the Day of atonement, which proves further that they did not regard Jesus' death as an atonement for the sins of mankind as claimed by Paul.

Why was Yeshua later portrayed as being in conflict with the Pharisees and not with the Sadducees? Hyam Maccoby explains that because by that time the Sadducees had lost any little religious authority they had and the Pharisees were its sole repository. As the Sadducees were known to be collaborators

---

[105] Matthew 27:25

with the Romans, it was very important to show that Yeshua had been a rebel not against them, which meant against the Roman occupation, but against Jewish religion. He states further that, *"The only Christian doctrines which would have been regarded as blasphemous by the Pharisees were those introduced by Paul sometime after his conversion. Before that, therefore, there can have been no clash between the Nazarenes and the Pharisees on religious grounds; though they may well have been conflicts between the Nazarenes and the High Priest on political grounds, since the High Priest, the quisling guardian of Roman interests, would certainly have regarded with suspicion a movement which still declared Jesus, a crucified rebel, as their leader."* It is only due to Paul's deviation and schism from the beliefs of these early Jewish followers of Yeshua or Nazarenes, his aggressively preaching the new religion he had unauthorizedly started – where faith in Jesus the Christ was a replacement for the Mosaic Law – that the Jews began to develop hostility and great contempt for those who gradually became known as Christians. The latter have also come to hate them for nearly two millennia[106]...

Maybe Jesus was a Pharisee, but Paul who claimed to be one was actually not one.

Paul claimed to his correspondents that he was a true-born Jew from a strict Pharisee background, but there are reasons to believe that he wrote like that only to increase his status in their eyes. *Acts* states that he had studied in the academy of the famous Pharisee leader Gamaliel (22:3), although Paul himself

---

[106] For instance, John Chrysostom (348-407), an early Church father, gave 8 sermons against the Jews and Judaizing Christians, where he said, *"I hate the Jews; they are possessed by the devil. Jewish religion is a disease... The pitiful and miserable Jews ... They are fit for slaughter... Certainly it is the time for me to show that demons dwell in the synagogue, not only in the place itself but also in the souls of the Jews ..."* (*On the Jews*) Martin Luther (1483-1546) wrote even worse things about the Jews. He recommended among other things that synagogues be burned, Jewish homes destroyed, and rabbis forbidden to teach under the threat of death. (Robert Kittel, *Theologians under Hitler* New Haven, Conn. Yale 1985)

does not say so. However, he states that he, as an enthusiastic Pharisee, was violently opposed to the young Yeshua movement which he persecuted under the orders of the High Priest, a Sadducee, who was bitterly and continuously opposed to the...Pharisees!? But if Yeshua's movement had been a religious heresy, it would not have been the High Priest's concern; moreover, if it had been opposed to the Pharisees, his own opponents, he would have been pleased. It is only because it was a Messianic political movement that he was concerned. The last person who would have been employed as part of his police force against revolutionaries would be a Pharisee, as they were in favor of those rebelling against Rome. So it is likely that Paul was not a Pharisee but an adventurer with some kind of post of police officer in the motley crew under the High Priest. Then *Acts* has him claim he was born a Roman citizen, then that he had voted the death of Christians, which means that he had been a member of the Sanhedrin, something Paul would have boasted about. It seems that Paul's insistence that he was a Pharisee was a decoy to claim a continuity between ancient and venerable Judaism and his new religion, Christianity, which is actually a very daring departure from the former and shocked its members as quite alien and without roots in it in spite of Paul's claims that the whole Torah was prefiguring Jesus. Paul's style of writing has nothing Pharisaic about it. There is nothing in his Epistles to prove that he was a Pharisee, but much to prove he was not one.

Not a unique figure

Most Christians believe that Jesus was a unique figure in his time, a one-of-a-kind preacher. Actually there were many itinerant preachers like him at this time, who were also gathering followers and preaching a messianic message; for instance, Apollonius of Tyana, a famous mystic also endowed with mystic powers. He was attracted to Pythagoras' teachings and wanted to go to its origin, India, as Pythagoras had done centuries earlier. So he travelled to India, where it is said that he met eighteen sages who taught him Vedic wisdom. He has been regularly compared to Jesus-Christ, including by 4th century

Christians. The most popular preacher was probably Yeshua's cousin, John the Baptist. In *Matthew* (3.11), Yeshua presents himself to him and is baptized. Baptism is understood by the Christians to be a ritual undergone to remove the stain of the so-called Original Sin, which was invented by Paul; but according to Christian dogma, Jesus-Christ was sinless and therefore should not have required this rite. This gospel states that John the Baptist recognized Yeshua as the promised savior, and yet, inexplicably, he did not become his follower but remained the leader of his own group!? If this event has any historical validity, it is apparent that Yeshua was probably a disciple of John the Baptist. He likely followed him for a while, and only became an independent religious leader after John's arrest and execution, or he may have assumed leadership of John's movement.

During the developing concept of the Christian god, many people were worshipping other gods. So there was an incentive to make one's god all-powerful and all-seeing, lest someone might claim that their god was more magnificent than yours. There was a mood of competition; it became a case of *"whatever your god can do, so can our do, and he can do it better; our god is more awesome than your god."* Thus it was common for all claimants to ascribe unlimited powers to their gods. The early followers of Jesus-Christ, in their converting zeal, may have attributed to him all kinds of wonderful, divine things so that he would look as good as the gods of the competitive religions and cults. The Gentiles had no conception of a Messiah. They would not accept anyone less than a god as their object of worship, so Jesus-Christ was divinized and "reborn" as "God". The wise second century Roman philosopher Celsus said of the Christian idea that other's religions are mythology and only theirs is factual, *"Are these distinctive happenings unique to the Christians, and if so, how are they unique? Ours are to be accounted myths, and theirs is to be believed? In truth there is nothing unusual in what the Christians believe, except they believe it to the exclusion of more comprehensive truths about God."*

No solid evidence

Whether Yeshua actually died on the cross and resurrected is questionable. But that he is God, God's Son and the only One, and that he died for the sins of the world does not rest on any other evidence than Paul's claims. Biases are well-known to be impossible to fully overcome, no matter how much one tries to minimize them. Unless one is a Christian who is already committed to the Bible and is so predisposed to believing Christian doctrines that one cannot look at the data objectively – and there is no such data except Paul's words – it is impossible to prove that Jesus-Christ was God's son, the unique one, God Himself, born from a virgin, and that he died for people's sins. You cannot accept as truths Paul's speculations just because we have records of his writings, or because he was an early writer and a zealous preacher who converted many people to accept his claims. These are not criterions of authenticity. We saw how many of his arguments are debunked concoctions. Paul's words are the only data and evidence. To accept his speculations at face value is blind, unquestioned faith. They are unsupported assertions. Where is the indisputable evidence of Jesus-Christ's divine nature? Or that he was more than a powerful religious preacher and reformer and a great devotee of God? The tendency to deify spiritual leaders is common in the East. Many Indian yogis endowed with mystic powers (*yoga-siddhis*), achieved through practicing severe austerities, perform what are called miracles and claim to be, or are acclaimed as *avatars* of God.

All the second century Christians seem to have thought that Yeshua had resurrected after his burial. Some thought he was divine, as per Paul's claims that he was God, God's only son, and that he died as an atonement for people' sins. Others did not accept him as such, nor believed that he had died for their sins and those of mankind. There were thus various currents in early Christianity, and soon fratricidal fighting began. Bishops took side and fought against each other virulently, including with armies, on theological issues. We can conclude that Christianity as we know it is not a religion directly given by God; it is a concocted religion. The proof: Yeshua's genuine disciples, which included his family members, objected from the beginning to Paul's concoctions. *His* ideas became a new religion, Christianity. It may have started with the life and teachings of Yeshua, but it has since been contaminated by the speculations of Paul and the self-serving manipulations of princes, emperors, popes and scribes.

Christianity is a religious syncretism.

Luke mentions shepherds coming to visit Yeshua at his birth. In Egyptian and Greek legends, they are symbols of the birth of the gods. In this way, ancient legends may have been christianized, as well as the teachings of Persian, Greek and Jewish philosophers. In addition to the shepherds of low social standing, *Matthew* 2 mentions rich wise men from the East bringing gifts of gold, frankincense and myrrh. *"Wherefrom in the East? East meant from the eastern side of the Jordan, which means the Jordanian deserts connecting with the Arabian deserts. Gold was mined in Arabia and frankincense and myrrh are harvested from trees that only grow in southern Arabia. Justin Martyr, a Palestinian Christian from Caesarea wrote in 160 that the wise men were from Arabia. He mentions this 5 times in a book called Dialogue with Trypho, the Jew. Tertullian and Clement of Rome affirmed the same location.*[107]

This duality of poor shepherds and rich men may simply be a symbol that Yeshua came both for the poor and the rich. And since the shepherds were Jews and the wise men were Gentiles, that he came for both. Dogma is only the hardening of myths into nonnegotiable truths. It is an interpretation of reality but not reality itself. Christianity claims to be unique and new, whereas it is the result of the syncretism of ancient religions it has

---

[107] Kenneth E. Bailey, *Jesus Through Middle Eastern Eyes*. SPCK, London 2008

forgotten. Genuine religion does not result in institutionalized violence. Apart from the attempt to put in practice the commandment of loving one's next, which pious Christians and the clergy especially tried to follow, besides the moral behavior expected of religious people (which was thoroughly lacking even in the clergy as attested by 6th century bishop Gregory of Tours, for instance) untold violence followed as we will see in chapter 9. For centuries, Europe was officially Christian but people did not really follow that religion. It was imposed to their subjects by the kings as they converted, but it was not a matter of personal choice and adherence to it did not go beyond paying lip service to it. What a tragedy to discover that our parents and forefathers' faith rests on the elucubrations of Saul of Tarsus, the so-called saint Paul, disguised as Jesus' religion! Paul must be still rotting in hell for all the atrocities committed in the name of Jesus for centuries by the followers of the religion he, Paul, invented.

The tragedy of Christianity

The confusion between Jesus-Christ and God Himself, created by Paul, makes it that the Christians do not develop genuine love for God. In other words, by turning Yeshua – a devotee of God and a spiritual teacher – into God Himself, all the love which is supposed to go to God, its proper object, is deviated towards Yeshua. It is not the authorized affection of disciples for their spiritual master, that Yeshua's direct disciples expressed, and that the master offers to God. From this, all the love supposed to go to God goes to Yeshua, and the figure of "God the father" – Lord Shri Krishna in the Vedic tradition – has been completely obscured and eclipsed. This is in my humble opinion the tragedy of Christianity: Paul cheated them of developing their eternal loving relationship of love with God by making Yeshua into God. The Jews worship their ancestral tribal deity, Yahweh, that they have gradually elevated to the status of the only true God. That does not make him into God, does it? The Muslims did the same. But the Christians do not worship a tribal deity made into God but a man made into God. That is the difference. Of course, along the centuries many sincere Christians – mystics, monks, nuns and laymen and women alike – have developed sincere affection for Jesus-Christ. One certainly gets some spiritual benefit by worshipping a great devotee of God like him, but it is not the same as if one worships and develops love for God Himself as taught by Yeshua. The Christians have been tricked by Paul into worshipping Yeshua – a saintly Jew who came to enlighten the Jews – as God, while blaming the Jews for killing God. How absurd! How sad!

Christians value Yeshua's death more than his life.

For modern Christians, the most important fact about Jesus-Christ is that he died for their sins, so if they believe in him, they can hope to spend eternity in heaven. His teachings are de-emphasized. *"The story of Christianity is the story of the beliefs that Jesus professed developing into the religion that professes Jesus. In other words; dogma. It is pure folly to believe that Simon Peter, Thomas, Mary Magdalene et al followed Jesus because, when he died, they would be able to absolve their sins by believing in him. This later theological construction was created by believers who were searching for a meaning to the seemingly pointless execution of their leader and teacher. Those who originally followed Jesus did so because of his life – because he was an exemplary teacher who radically reinterpreted the Law in favor of inclusion rather than exclusion. Those who now follow Jesus do so because of his death. They turn a man's poignant teachings – his life's work – into a secondary and near meaningless preface to the panacea of his death. We primarily have Paul and John the evangelist (two people who did not know Jesus in his life) to thank for this inexcusable dumbing-down of Jesus' life. With Paul and John's help, what Christianity would become is embodied in the*

Nicene Creed. Take a look at it. Dogmatic fiat has expurgated everything the man stood for."[108]

The book of Revelation and the misinterpretation of Scripture

Modern Christians consider the *Book of Revelation* to be about the end of the world. This is not the case. The book is principally about what the author considered to be the end of *his* world, specifically the fall of Jerusalem to the Romans in AD 70, with the Temple being burned down and countless Jews killed. It was the end of the world for those Jewish followers of Yeshua who had expected him to return and restore the holy land to God's "chosen people". What happened was the exact opposite of these expectations. The author was trying to rally the Jews and present his vision that God would soon return to destroy the Romans and restore the Kingdom of the Jews. The reference to an Antichrist is a metaphor for the Roman Emperor, Nero, and the number 666 spells out Nero's imperial name with the Jewish numerology system. The author did not feel safe at the time to actually spell out Nero's name. So, in essence, the *Book of Revelation* is a lamentation for the disaster at Jerusalem, a call to rally the Jews to a brighter future, and a screed against the 'demonic' Romans, the Four Horsemen of the Apocalypse. Elaine Pagels, one of the world's leading biblical scholars did extensive research to untangle the mystical nature of this book. Moreover, Yeshua himself, who is usually portrayed as meek, humble and loving, appears in Revelation as quite gory too: *"From his mouth comes a sharp two-edge sword with which to strike down the nations"* (19:11-21). *"He holds a sharp sickle in his hand and the blood flows as high as a horse's bridle for 200 miles"* (14:14-21).

---

[108] http://trevorburrus.newsvine.com/_news/2008/03/05/1345329- 10-reasons-why-christianity-is-wrong

Salvation is not the ultimate goal of religion.

Many Christians are now open to the idea that there is some truth in all religions and therefore they tolerate them, but they claim that theirs is the only true one, the only one which can grant salvation, so they do not give equal respect to the other religious traditions.[109] But actually salvation is not the ultimate goal of religion. Pure love of God and eternal loving service to Him are; salvation is an automatic by-product of pure love for God. Christians have no information whatsoever about the spiritual world, neither about "heaven", the higher heavenly planets of delights, and do not know the distinction between both. They do not know that pure love of God is the mentality and condition of all the inhabitants of the spiritual world, and that if one wants at all to go there one needs to develop it. Christians assume and claim that the Christian West is superior to all other people because they believe that Christianity is the only true religion and all others are heathens worshipping "false gods". It is quite naïve, however, to think that it is only through Yeshua that a path to God has been historically opened for the first time two thousand years ago, whereas the world is billions and trillions of years old. The path has always been opened since creation. God's doors are opened to all sincere spiritualists. No religion has the monopoly of the access to the Godhead.

Again, the importance of beliefs cannot be over- emphasized. If you believe that you are a soul and identify yourself as such, you will want to live more and more on that level; you will endeavor to develop your spiritual side. If you believe God is not a distant, semi-impersonal and indifferent Being who is a father figure but

---

[109] "While followers of other religions can receive divine grace, it is also certain that objectively speaking they are in a gravely deficient situation in comparison with those who, in the Church, have the fullness of the means of salvation." *Dominus Jesus*, §22, 2000

also a terrible judge, but you understand Him as a very near, loving Being, the eternal lover of the soul, you will want to develop that relationship with Him. Instead of treating mercilessly your fellow human beings and trying to exploit them in various ways, you will want to share this knowledge with them and treat them with the kindness and respect due to them as souls and servants of the same loving Father, Friend and Beloved. Fortunately, we see countless people raised in Christianity realizing its severe limitations and not cantoning themselves to dogmatic religion.

Chapter nine
A dark history

Martyrs

Any Christian will tell you that in the early years of their religion Christians were persecuted by the Romans and thrown to the lions by these "pagans". It is true that up to two thousand of them were killed by the Romans, much less than they like to make out. However, the reason why any Christians were persecuted at all was not because of their religion – as the Romans tolerated and pretty much absorbed all religions, seeing their various deities as protectors of their empire – but because the Christians refused to honor the Emperor, which was seen as seditious. In Gibbon's *Decline and Fall of the Roman Empire*, it is estimated that a total number of one thousand five hundred Christians were killed by the Romans in the more populous and Christian East. Perhaps another five hundred died in the West. But they themselves persecuted much more people once they obtained political power: *"In its heyday the Christian Churches practiced routine persecution. They tortured, mutilated, branded, dismembered and killed as a matter of course. They condemned to death any who questioned their dogmas. They burned Jews, heretics, apostates and "pagans" in large numbers. They imagined enemies everywhere and had them exterminated. Among their countless victims were women whose chief crimes seem to have been living alone, looking old, keeping pets, and knowing something about herbs and midwifery. Christians even persecuted their fellow believers. It is sobering to reflect that over almost 2000 years Christians have never been persecuted by any of their supposed enemies as viciously as they have been persecuted by fellow Christians."*[110]

---

[110] http://www.badnewsaboutchristianity.com/he0_present.htm

Christian persecution

"The Christian period is more atrocious than all the preceding periods of mankind all together."[111] The God of Yeshua is a God of compassion and love who looks upon humanity with benevolence and mercy. His representatives were far from doing so as soon as they got political power, and during centuries, as any study of the spreading of Christianity will unfortunately reveal. The Neoplatonist philosopher Porphyry (233-309 AD) wrote, *"The gods have proclaimed Christ to have been most pious, but the Christians are a confused and vicious sect."* Paradoxically, the Christians imposed Jesus-Christ's message of love with the greatest brutality and violence. There were persecutions of other brands of Christianity deemed heretical because they did not follow the "party line", force conversion or death under torture, total intolerance towards the worshipers of the demigods in the Roman empire, killing them and destroying their temples, officially outlawing them, and persecution of the Jews when they were not indispensable – In French history, when the Muslims became the masters of the Mediterranean Sea, trade suffered immensely; gold became rare and the Jews were given favors because they were the only caste of traders left, selling even slaves to the Muslims. Violence was rampant during the Spanish and Portuguese conquests, including Goa in India, with Inquisition cruelty applied to people considered as savages but still expected to follow Christianity and tortured if they did not. There was also the Amerindian genocide and even Hitler justified his crusade against the Jews as a catholic doing his duty against God's enemies, Jesus' killers.

Anyone who did not agree with their creed, or their particular version of his history and mission, was branded as a heretic and excommunicated if not tortured and/or killed, like during the infamous times of the so-called "Holy" Inquisition. There were many barbaric atrocities perpetrated under the auspices of

---

[111] Frederic Daumer, *Secrets of Christian antiquity*, 1847

Christianity.[112] The Catholic Popes are infamous throughout a good part of history for being corrupt, even murderers and generally debauched, as much of the clergy.[113] As a result of Christian superstitions about the devil, demons, witches, etc. so many millions of innocent people were tortured to death in the most horrific fashion. Often, after facing hellish torture, the victims would be burned alive in the name of the Christian God. *"For the first three centuries the Church was relatively powerless and did little harm. It taught brotherhood, tolerance, peace, love, justice, mercy, and so on, to the extent of encouraging Christian soldiers to desert the Imperial armies. For the next 1500 years it was extremely powerful and harmful throughout Europe. It caused division, persecution, war, hatred, and injustice, and practiced the most spectacular viciousness and brutality... It has abused its power and opposed legal, political and educational reform. It has also opposed liberties and human rights... For many centuries the Church maintained its position by a combination of fraud [114] and*

---

[112] In 1545, the Christian "missionary" Francis Xavier wrote to the Pope asking for an inquisition to be held in Goa, the Christian foothold in India. The Pope agreed. More than a million Hindus were tortured and murdered simply because they followed a different religion. The inquisitor's first act was forbidding Hindus from practising their faith. *"The condemned Hindus were publicly burned at the stake in the square outside the Sé Cathedral in batches during ceremonies known as auto da fé (act of faith, in Portuguese)... Brahmins were nailed to crosses and beheaded to spread fear into the local populations...Many Hindu temples were converted or destroyed, and Christian churches built in their place, often from the materials of the temples they replaced... Hindu texts were burned in an effort to saturate the area with Christian religious texts...People that were accused of heresy were subjected to gruesome punishment...flogged, interrogated, and dismembered in front of relatives....* (Wikipedia)

[113] Pope Gregory I (509-604) introduced a celibacy edict to prevent property from passing from the Church to wives, families or mistresses of clergy. Thousands of babies were drowned in a pond outside the Lateran palace after the edict was issued.

[114] Like the so-called Constantine donation, for instance, a forged document claiming that Emperor Constantine I had given the whole of the Western Roman Empire to the Roman Catholic Church in the 4th century out of gratitude for having been miraculously cured of leprosy by Pope Sylvester I..

terror...Christian Churches were wholly responsible for the deaths of millions whose only crime was to dissent from their current version of orthodoxy."[115]

The Christians like to present Jesus-Christ as the prince of peace. However, go back a couple of hundred years to when the Church held total political supremacy: these Christians were happy to go around committing genocide in his name. In Europe and the Americas, the most fearful and superstitious time was when Christianity was at its height - up to the early 18th century. A little known fact is that the founding fathers of the American Republic rejected Christianity. One of them, John Adams, wrote of the Bible's content, *"Millions of fables, tales, legends, have been blended with both the Jewish and Christian revelation that have made them the bloodiest religion that has ever existed."* Thomas Jefferson, the author of the American Declaration of Independence back in the 1770s, wrote, *"Millions of innocent men, women and children, since the introduction of Christianity, have been burned, tortured, fined, imprisoned, yet we have not advanced one inch towards uniformity. What has been the effect of this coercion? To make one half of the world fools, the other half hypocrites, to support roguery and error all over the earth..."* James Madison concurred and stated, *"The last fifteen hundred years have resulted in more or less all places in pride and indolence in the clergy, ignorance and servility in the laity; in both, superstition, bigotry and persecution."* These founding fathers of America were saying that the religion of their upbringing, Christianity, was full of superstition, fabrication, ignorance, fanaticism, and was also responsible for the torture, murder and enslavement of millions of human beings. Their idea was to set up in the new world of the Americas an ideal state free from its influence. They were masons and 'deists', that is they believed in God, but not in Christianity.

"The conduct of God, who disposes all things kindly, is to put religion into the mind by reason, and into the heart by grace. But to will to put it into the mind and heart by force and threats is not

---

[115] http://www.badnewsaboutchristianity.com/he0_present.htm

to put religion there, but terror."[116] Now, in the Western world, thanks to the arrival of the eighteenth century "Age of Reason", the Churches have lost most of their political power. So, if they do not torture anyone anymore, it is only because they have lost their power, since the powerful Church's establishment was challenged by determined men. Of course, notwithstanding this fact, the Church was dedicated for centuries to helping the poor and the sick, collecting and paying ransoms for Westerners enslaved by the Mohammedans, and was in charge of education. Nowadays it preaches again love and peace like in the first centuries. There is no question that that is so much better than their old ways. Mark Twain wrote, *"There is one notable thing about our Christianity: bad, bloody, merciless, money-grabbing, and predatory as it is – in our country particularly and in all other Christian countries in a somewhat modified degree – it is still a hundred times better than the Christianity of the Bible... Measured by our Christianity of to-day, bad as it is, hypocritical as it is, empty and hollow as it is, neither the Deity nor his Son is a Christian... Ours is a terrible religion. The fleets of the world could swim in spacious comfort in the innocent blood it has spilled.* [117]

In 313, the Edict of Milan of Emperor Constantine and his eastern counterpart Licinius gave Christianity a legal status, officially recognizing it as a legal religion. That Edict expressly granted religious liberty not only to the Christians, but to all religions, *"for the sake of the peace of our times, that each one may have the free opportunity to worship as he pleases; this regulation is made that we may not seem to detract from any dignity of any religion."* Constantine tolerated "paganism" and other religions, but he actively promoted Christianity, not as an act of genuine Christian faith but to create an alliance with the Christian god, whom he considered the most powerful deity. He was more concerned about social stability and the protection of

---

[116] Blaise Pascal, 1623-1662

[117] *"Mark Twain's Autobiography Set for Unveiling, a Century After His Death"* PBS News Hour 2010.

the empire from the wrath of the Christian god than he was about justice or care for the Christians. The Romans were obsessed with seeking the gods' intervention to avoid unfavorable consequences, so that the state could become stable because, it was thought, the forces of evil would be more balanced. Emperor Constantine, who killed his wife and son, saw in Christianity a pragmatic means of bolstering his own military power, conquering dissention and uniting the vast and troubled Roman Empire. The Church reaped enormous gains by compromising its ideology and prevalent beliefs. In 319, Constantine passed a law excusing the clergy from paying taxes or serving in the army. In 325, he summoned and presided over the council of Nicaea, which he organized according to the rules of the Senate. That first council was called by him to try to pacify and unite all Christians. He wanted to settle controversies and establish a consensus. There were very many Christians of his time that did not believe that Yeshua was anything but a messenger sent by God. They did not believe that he was the son of God neither God Himself. At that first council, Constantine brought together the two main factions at the time: the faction that believed in Yeshua as a messenger and those that believed that he was much more than that, the Pauline/Johannine faction. Though many church leaders compromised to fit in with the emperor's instructions, several did not. They were threatened and some of them then expelled. The heretical ideas of Paul – which were disagreed upon by many if not most genuine early Christians – were forced upon them at that first council.
The Neoplatonic philosopher Plotinus (205-270) also influenced early Christianity with his triune concept of the One, the Spirit and the Soul, his monistic vision of the One and his ideal of *henosis*, mystical union with the One, the Source. Many fundamental dogmatic changes were thus made to the Christian religion. The dogma of the Holy Trinity was concocted at that time as a compromise between those who thought Yeshua was a saintly man who had resurrected, and Paul's followers who claimed he was God Himself who incarnated. However, by trying to make a compromise which would accommodate various factions warrying about Yeshua's humanity versus his divinity,

or how much human and how much divine he was, the wording of the Nicene creed ended up with an oxymoron: *"fully God and fully man"*, which has become the Christian creed ever since!? However, the issue was not solved for many more centuries and divided the Church into many branches. Paul the heretic thus convinced the entire Christian world to believe in a vision he had over what Yeshua himself had taught. Nobody follows Yeshua today. Instead they follow what Paul wrote and the writings of four supposed disciples, who went to their deaths unaware that Gospels would be written in their names and then edited by many hands...

So that the Roman emperor would back the religion, it was accepted that only two entities were to be worshipped: the new 'Holy Trinity' and the emperor himself. The ideal was 'one empire, one emperor – Constantine – one religion – of which Constantine had complete control – and only one god – of whom Constantine was the representative. The Church was like a department in his empire. He radically altered it to fit in with his imperial political and "pagan" ideals, and the Christians by and large accepted his changes because their religion was to be made the official religion of the empire. In 355, bishops were exempted from ever being tried in secular courts, and in 378 an imperial decree stated that the Popes were above the law. Constantine himself did not "convert" until on his death-bed, where he accepted Arian and not Catholic Christian baptism. In 380, Christianity was made the official religion of the Roman empire under Emperor Theodosius I. Paul's new religion thus got political power, and it was imposed by the force of arms as a truth on everyone. From persecuted, the Catholic cult members became the persecutors, killing the so-called "pagans" and destroying all the temples of other faiths. In 382, the Church law declaring that "all heretics must be killed" was introduced. These so-called "heretics" were Christians who dared to follow a different style of Christianity than the authorized Roman version. The Theodosian laws made it illegal to disagree with the Church. In 391, Theodosius banned all religions from the empire apart from Christianity, on penalty of death. Much of the rapid growth of early Christianity was not achieved through a competition of ideas or by an evidence-based proselytizing effort, but rather by the overtaking of "pagan" shrines and places of worship. After killing or torturing its priests, Christians would take over a "pagan" shrine, usually on a hilltop, and convert it into a church, or demolish it and build a church with the same materials. Therefore, many Christian churches have underneath it a "pagan" shrine.[118]

As Christianity became more mundane, many sincere followers of Yeshua wanted to really apply his teachings and escaped political influence by retiring in the deserts of Egypt, Israel, Syria and Iraq, like the early Therapeutics, and founding communities. The lay communities slowly disappeared as the desert is not the best place to raise families and crops. Only monastic communities remained, some for centuries, and many ascetics lived lonely lives devoted to prayer. They became known as "the Fathers of the desert", who have left many precious writings, sharing their insights born from their exclusive devotion to spirituality. They inspired European monks who evangelized the various parts of Europe. When crusades to keep access to Jerusalem open for pilgrims were no longer practical, 'religious wars' between different Christian denominations followed, principally from 1524-1651, but continuing, in one way or another, until our days – for example, the conflict between Northern and Southern Ireland. When a religious war against another nation was not

---

[118] There are Black "Madonnas" (300 in France, 50 in Spain, 30 in Italy, 19 in Germany). They are connected to ancient goddesses, as almost all are found on the sites of pre-Christian, "pagan" shrines. (Isis of Egypt, Diana of Rome, Cybele of the Middle East are often black.) The worship of Isis, especially, which was the official religion of Egypt during Jesus' times, was spread around the Mediterranean Sea. A lot of elements of her religion, iconography and symbols have been reported on Mary such as redemption and salvation, baptism with water, names like Star of the sea, Queen of heaven, standing on the moon, with stars around her head, Mother and child (Horus). The black Madonna of Le Puy in France was originally a statue of Isis. Isis is also associated with Mary Magdalene (50 places of worship around the Mediterranean Sea, with also a shrine dedicated to the Black Madonna, especially in Marseille, where 3 are found.)

expedient, atrocities against Jews, in the form of expulsions (from Spain in 1492), Inquisitions[119], pogroms, and wholesale extermination, could help pump up the spirit of the faithful. This bloody past has been acknowledged at the highest level of Christian authority. In June of 1995 the Chicago Tribune reported that Pope John Paul II had urged the Roman Catholic Church to seize the "particularly propitious" occasion of the new millennium to recognize "the dark side of its history." In a 1994 confidential letter to cardinals which was later leaked to the Italian press, he asked, *"How can one remain silent about the many forms of violence perpetrated in the name of the faith – wars of religion, tribunals of the Inquisition and other forms of violations of the rights of persons?"*

Everyone is individually responsible for his spiritual life. You just cannot mechanically become a follower. That is what makes the Christian Church so unattractive, the followers are not enlightened at all. They simply do things, "because my father did it" or because the priest or pastor said it, or they are simply going through the motions of being part of a religious community. But they do not have much conviction, therefore they cannot stand on it. Everything becomes just a club or an institution. Very few Christians are real Christians today. Their religion is failing in a *de facto* sense, although it might appear to be growing on paper. It is flawed in its limited spirituality and logical inconsistency. The Christians know that they have a father in heaven, but it is a father that they have never met nor can they ever hope to meet, due to lack of knowledge about Him and of a practical method to develop love for Him. Still, everyone wants to believe he will go to "heaven". Their faith is mired in problems. It has become a casual religion. The commitment of the people is less and the services of the religion are also less. The more the world is projected into modern times, the less binding the link between the common man and his faith. Today,

---

[119] The Conversos (Jews forcibly converted to Christianity but suspected of practicing their original religion) were hunted like dogs by Spanish and Portuguese Inquisitions for over 350 years.

successful religious organizations have degenerated into big propaganda machines doing business in the name of God and simply cheating the people. Through radio and television networks they provide people with a sense of belonging in a world increasingly plagued by impersonalism and voidism. Most of the times, they deliver to their members some sort of emotional impact with live "miracles", which they equate with spiritual experience. Such bogus religious groups are often a one-man preaching organization; the preacher is working for his personal benefit, making a show of religiosity; he is nothing more than a glorified entertainer. Many of those flamboyant show-bottle moralizers are involved in sex scandals. Still, the people respond and the religious organizations receive vast sums of money. Whatever, the Christian religion is still now something of a bulwarks against atheism. It will be sorely needed as civilization continues to crumble.

Chapter ten

Yeshua's different roles

We can distinguish different roles in Jesus. First, his role as a revolutionary, which has been eclipsed. In the frame of his revolutionary "political" career as a messiah claimant, Yeshua taught the people, sometimes crowds, about the "Kingdom of God". He taught them to behave in a righteous way, to strictly follow the Torah in order to attract God's mercy and usher in the Messianic days.

From the available "historical" material, Yeshua seems to fit well in the category of the Jewish prophets. He was definitely a great devotee of God and as such had mystic powers, which he allegedly used to heal and perform "miracles" to create faith in his message. He prophesized many things, so there is his role as a prophet. Unfortunately, the most important part of what he foresaw did not happen, as we saw earlier. His performing miracles, if he did, were not a particular proof of divinity as misunderstood. Yogis and highly elevated spiritualists in India perform the same kind of miracles. If he performed them, it was simply to create faith in his message.

Then there is Jesus as what Paul made of him, as what we have been led to believe by a sleigh of hand all his disciples saw him like. It is another role which manifested later in spite of him, after his crucifixion, but that role is a role that the self-appointed apostle Paul has unauthorizedly invented and attributed to him when he replaced the original human, Jewish revolutionary Jesus by a divine and mythical Christ. Paul gave the term 'messiah' a completely different meaning, foreign to Jewish culture.

Yeshua had a fourth role: he was also a spiritual revolutionary, an exalted rabbi, a teacher addressing crowds but also guiding personally a restricted number of disciples in their spiritual development. So that was his role as a spiritual master or *guru*.[120] But by doing so, we should not think that he was creating a separate religion. So in that sense, whether one identifies himself as a Christian or not, as a member of the Church or not, one can try to follow Yeshua's spiritual teachings as recorded in the Gospels. He inaugurated a kind of spiritual communism, putting everything in common, to fight against greed and attachment and to simplify one's life in order to dedicate to developing love for God. He spoke of renunciation for cultivation of divine love.

Did Yeshua ever go to India?

There are long-standing traditions, both Muslim and others, that Yeshua survived crucifixion and lived in the Middle East and India. Indians also deny his death on the cross, saying that he feigned death by his mystic powers, or entered in yogic trance, and that he survived crucifixion.[121] P. Yogananda, one of the early pioneers of *yoga* in the USA, wrote about it too in his writings, although he insists to portray Yeshua strangely both as a monist mystic and as a cosmic principle he calls "Christ consciousness"...*The Passover Plot* [122] was among the first book to popularize the theory that Jesus did not die while on the cross. The book *Jesus died in Kashmir* [123] describes that Paul did not have a vision of Yeshua but actually saw him on the Damascus caravan road. After having been healed for around a year, Yeshua was on his way back to India, where he had already spent some of the nearly twenty years of his life between his early adolescence and the age of about thirty. Yeshua is said to have died there, in Kashmir, in Srinagar, where his tomb with the

---

[120] En relisant les Evangiles, Arnaud Desjardins, Véronique Loiseleur, La Table ronde, Paris, 1990

[121] *"He was only injured and after treatment returned to India where he actually died."* (K.S. Sudarshan, nationalist Hindu leader, 2007 speech, mentioned in Worldwide religious news website.)

[122] Schonfield, Hugh, Bantam Books, New York 1965

[123] A. Faber-Kaiser 1977

inscription in Hebrew *"Tomb of Yeshua"* can be found. We just saw above that, according to *The Bible Fraud*, it was Yeshua's twin. The same book claims that himself travelled to France and England where he allegedly died by stoning at the hands of Jews in Lud... There have been adherents to a core idea of a bloodline of Jesus through Mary Magdalen for a very long time. The belief that she travelled with a group of companions to the south of France and was the wife of Yeshua was a widely and deeply held belief in southern France and England for several centuries. So, in different traditions, whether Indian, Muslim, British or French, we have the idea that Yeshua did not die on the cross but travelled out of Palestine. I am not developing the theme here of whether he travelled Eastward or Westward, as it is not my purpose.

Vegetarian master and disciples

The writings of early Christian fathers show that many of Yeshua's early followers were vegetarian. Clement of Alexandria (1st century) wrote, *"Matthew partook of seeds, nuts and vegetables, abstaining from flesh"* and *"Peter said, 'I live on olives and bread to which I only rarely add vegetables.'"* The early Christian writer Hegesippus wrote that Yeshua's brother James *"drank no wine...nor ate no living thing; even his clothes were free from any taint of death..."* Augustine confirms that James *"lived on seeds and vegetables and did not accept meat or wine"*. Many of the earliest Christians were strict vegetarians, as they were followers of Yeshua, the Nazarene. (Nazarenes and the similar Essenes sect of Judaism were strict vegetarians). According to some scholars, the name 'Jesus of Nazareth' is a mistranslation. Some say that the village called Nazareth did not exist before a couple of hundred years after Yeshua.

Paul compromised with the strictness of the Mosaic law and the vegetarian diet of Yeshua and his disciples to make it easier for non-Jews to come to the fold. He concentrated his preaching efforts on them, which earned him the title of "Apostle of the Gentiles". The Romans were not vegetarians, so to suit them, vegetarianism was completely downplayed. References from the

Bible regarding vegetarianism were removed when the Roman Emperors took control of the religion. During Emperor Theodosius's reign, in the 5th century, Patriarch Timothy in Egypt made meat-eating compulsory on Sundays for all priests, to stamp out Gnostic and similar saintlier, ascetic vegetarian priests and monks. The official Church frowned on vegetarianism, a mood carried on to this day, with some Christians claiming that *"Vegetarianism is from the devil"*. But can one really mentally picture Yeshua, a most loving and compassionate personality, slitting a lamb or a calf's throat so he can gorge on its flesh, the blood dripping down his long flowing, white robes?

Chapter 11

Why I stopped being a Christian but did not become an atheist

To believe in God is a natural thing, and any child naturally believes in Him. It is only by bad association with agnostic or atheistic people while growing up that one may lose this natural understanding of the benevolent divine origin of everything. Atheists are like gay people in the sense that a small minority insists for their perversions and deviations to become acknowledged as being as valid as the normal behavior which has characterized mankind for time immemorial. Relativists rightfully reject the Christian claim of inerrancy of the Bible, which states that the Bible should be taken at face value, as free from error in everything it affirms, no matter how contradictory[124] or downright immoral it may appear. The paucity of reliable knowledge in the scriptures of the three

---

[124] For instance, *Genesis* presents two separate stories of creation, side by side, which cannot be harmonized; they are incompatible, as it could not have literally happened both ways.

Semitic religions may also make one question them altogether. The ancient sacred Vedic literature of India, the Vedas, offer by contrast time-tested knowledge. Their presentation of God, of creation, of material energy and of the nature of the self is complete and unchallenged. The atheists seem to have chosen to argue with the weakest among the few theistic systems so as to cast doubt on all theistic philosophies. Let them become acquainted with higher theistic philosophical systems like the ancient Vedic ones and study them. Then let them have a dialogue or a debate with Vedic philosophers, not just with Christian apologists who are usually ill-equipped due to their mostly faith-based approach – although some have presented an excellent reason-based and real-science-based defense of theism to counteract atheistic pseudo-scientific propaganda.[125] The human condition is to live simultaneously both temporal and eternal truths, and, although there is an innate transcendent aspect to the existence and personality of the human soul, deprived of proper guidance, many people become disillusioned by theism. They may in time become desperate and lose hope to find a spiritual solution to their problems. They then usually exclusively turn to matter and become fascinated by it. They become so dazzled by the enjoyment it affords, although it is so meagre and short-lived, that they come to conceive matter as the only reality or the most important thing. Their disappointment with and often subsequent opposition to Christianity have pushed them to do away with the very idea of God, and they then imagine that this world is self-manifested. They have thrown the baby with the bath water and developed over time all kinds of unscientific, worthless, materialistic and atheistic philosophies based on unsound logic and conclusions, such as positivism[126],

---

[125] *I don't have enough faith to become an atheist,* Norman L. Geisler and Frank Turek, Crossway books, 2004. And *Stealing from God,* Frank Turek, NavPress 2014

[126] A. Comte (1795-1857), who propounded positivism, held that thinking about God was the infancy of thought, philosophical thoughts its childhood, and resolute moral thinking its maturity.

secularism, pessimism, existentialism, agnosticism, relativism, etc., which have led astray countless unfortunate ignorant victims or pushed them to skepticism or nihilism. But atheism is not a positive alternative to Christianity at all. Its theories destroy the sacredness of life. Atheism is simply the envious, proud and ungrateful denial of God's right of authorship and proprietorship on everything and everyone. Atheism is a foolish, illogical and untenable philosophical stance.

The subject of the Vedas is the Absolute Truth, the Supreme Personality, God. He is said to be full of love as well as being the original object of love. That means He is the natural object of service, as true love always translates into actions performed for the pleasure of the beloved. Why is God lovable? Because He has all the qualities attracting us to another being to the superlative degree – beauty, knowledge, power, wealth, fame and detachment. He is therefore most attractive, which owes Him His main name, "Krishna", coming from the root *karsan*, to attract, and *na*, the most, meaning "the most attractive being" in Sanskrit. Since He is full of bliss, anyone who comes in contact with Him through loving service, which is one's natural eternal function, participates in that bliss.

Let us take a look at the process of comparative philosophy. Philosophy mainly addresses the question of what is the origin of everything; in other words, what is the primeval cause of all causes. A philosophical concept is classified according to its explanation of that original cause, and a philosophy according to its highest concept of that cause. The proof of a higher concept is that it more fully explains reality and has basis in that reality. Philosophical concepts may be divided into theistic and atheistic. Theism means to conceive the cause of all causes as being the Absolute, described as an all-powerful unique, divine Person, God. Atheism means any philosophy that is opposed to that conception; for instance, the conception that life evolves from matter organizing itself through an evolutionary process, like Darwinism; the conception that the ultimate reality is a complete void, like Buddhism; or the conception that the Absolute is not a person, God, but is impersonal and formless, like in Judaism and monistic Hindu *Advaita-vedanta*. Theism is clearly a higher concept. Why so? Because atheism relies on a false and illogical principle according to which something comes from nothing. The cause of all causes is also, per definition, the origin of consciousness, personality and desire. Atheism fails to explain the original cause of those. Therefore, because it explains more fully reality and moreover is rooted in that reality, theism is definitely a higher concept.

The Vedas do not teach that God has created the human beings in the material world along with all the other species. They explain that the souls are not created but are eternal, which means coexistent with God. They are small units of consciousness and as such possess free will. They are manifested by God at the border region between the material and the spiritual worlds. There they are given the choice between serving Him, which they know to be their eternal natural function, or being indifferent to His service. The souls who make the proper use of their free will by accepting their eternal function of loving service to Him are elevated to the spiritual dimension, His blissful abode. There they enjoy, in a spiritual body similar to His and His eternal associates', the unlimited happiness coming from their personal sweet relationship of loving service to Him. For those souls who neglect His service due to a separatist mentality and misuse their free will by choosing to seek happiness independently from Him, in His unfathomably unconditional love He has created this material world to give them an opportunity to try to do so, along with a reformatory and emancipatory process revealed in the *Vedas*. They fall from their pristine state of purity into that lower sphere made of material energy, which has a tremendous power of illusion on their consciousness and makes them forget their identity as eternal souls, as well as their relationship with wonderful God. They become covered by two envelopes, one gross, one subtle, a material body and a mind, and identify themselves fully with those coverings. Not functioning as souls, which means as loving servants of God, they cannot enjoy the happiness coming from that relationship. Since the souls have an inherent happy nature like God, of whom they are parts and parcels, they naturally look for happiness, but under the spell of illusion they look for it outside of their relationship with God. They are inevitably committing negative or sinful activities and entangling themselves in the maze of actions and their reactions, enjoying and suffering in the karmic cycle of repeated births and deaths.

It is not that God creates everything *ex nihilo* (from zero) and then matter, space and time arise from nothing. Those two latter ones are interconnected. Time exists in space. The *Vedas* teach that both are eternal. In his 1905 theory of relativity, A. Einstein taught that they cannot really be separated and spoke of the space-time continuum. This is also the conception in quantum physics. Like space, time is said to have two aspects: *nitya*-kala, eternal time, which is experienced in the higher dimension, the spiritual space, and *jada-kala*, its reflection, which is experienced in the mundane sphere or material space. The ancient Greeks also inherited from the Vedas this dual conception of time, *aion*, sacred or eternal time, and *chronos*, ordinary time. Many people in the West think that philosophy began with the Greeks, that for the Greek thinkers everything was unknown and there were the first to ponder over many questions. However, they were asking the same questions which preoccupied their predecessors, preoccupy us and will continue to preoccupy all further generations of human beings. The old link between Greece and India had slackened with the passage of time and they did not confirm anymore their search with the Vedic revelation. Their religion had been reduced to demigod worship. The spreading westward of atheistic Buddhism had also influenced them. They had become more or less empiric independent thinkers and had established an official academy of empiric philosophy.

The universe is made of matter, and observation shows that everything material usually goes through six phases: it appears, grows, stabilizes, has by-products, dwindles and disappears due the law of entropy, the second law of Thermodynamics. Indeed, the universe had undoubtedly a beginning. It may be gigantic but since everything which has a beginning is contingent to an earlier cause, it can be deducted that it is a gigantic effect of a cause which must be tremendously powerful to have been able to produce it. That cause cannot be blind natural laws and material forces, because those are components and characteristics of the universe itself, they are not preexistent to it. So logically that cause must be a metaphysical or spiritual force. We think that "seeing is believing" but "metaphysical" literally means "beyond the simple laws of physics"; this implies that it is not empirically verifiable. It refers to another dimension, the features of which are inconceivable by ordinary conventional means.

It is supernatural, which means literally "beyond nature", which indicates that it is beyond matter and material time. One could then ask what is the cause of that cause itself. However, the principle of cause and effect applies only to temporary contingent things, not to what is beyond time and matter. That would take us to a *regressum ad infinitum* argument. If it is beyond time, it is what is called eternal. Eternal means ever-existing, not coming into being, not becoming; it means uncreated, not produced by a prior cause. Moreover, that powerful cause must be intelligent. Logic dictates that not only something does not come from nothing, but also that nothing exists without sufficient reason and purpose. Is that the "God of the philosophers"? Well, it sure doesn't look like Yahweh, the tribal biblical deity, but it is God nonetheless. Atheists try to wiggle out of these simple and logical principles by word-jugglery and absurd theories, but they can only cheat and convince those who want to be cheated. By the way, one of the most important texts of the Vedic literature, the *Bhagavad-gita*, describes two natures found in this world, a divine one and a demoniac one, and clearly explains that one of the manifestations or symptoms of the demoniac one is the denial of God's existence, atheism (16:8). It is only by God's grace, coming through a genuine spiritual guide that one can qualify to understand transcendental truth, never through material knowledge, science, mundane logic and arguments. How can man understand an immeasurable entity with his limited intelligence? Another kind of knowledge is necessary. When God is pleased by one's service attitude, the power to know is bestowed by His mercy upon man's faculties, assisting him to understand. He states Himself in the *Bhagavad-gita* that He can only be known through love, that is loving service or *bhakti*.

It is perfectly logical to conclude that it is God who has made universal and eternal ethical and moral laws valid for all times and all peoples, the general rules governing what is appropriate and inappropriate human behavior. All these ethical guidelines and rules are so designed by God for our individual and collective benefit. God has written these standards in every human being's heart. This is natural and rational theology. The Swiss protestant theologian Emil Brunner made an ever stronger statement, *"There is no such thing as 'the Moral' in itself - as the 'autonomous' ethic says there is - that is, something which is 'Moral' in and for itself, that which is 'morally Good,' understood as independent of the will of God. That which is morally 'good' is identical with that which is determined by the will of God."*[127]

Due to the practical application of modern science in their daily lives, people have developed great faith in it, so much so that a myth of so-called irrefutable scientific knowledge has been built. Indeed, science has produced amazing things, but atheistic scientists are "selling" their unproven reductionist theories to an unsuspecting public, and before people know, they have imbibed them and accepted them as truths. Those scientists are not just presenting them as theories or avenues of exploration but

---

[127] *The Christian doctrine of God.* p.166

aggressively pushing them as gospel truths like Evangelist preachers push their wares. Cloaked in the prestigious dress of science, borrowing its original respectability built by early theistic scientists like Copernicus, Kepler, Newton, Faraday, Einstein, Born or Heisenberg, they are advancing their subversive pawns on the chessboard of human society, pushing it towards the abyss of nescient Godlessness. The new or modern culture based on a pseudo-scientific reductionist view of life can only lead to complete hedonism, and the result of such a materialistic outlook is clearly demonstrated in today's world. It is obviously taken as a license for a life of unrestricted selfishness devoted to the gratification of one's senses and mind. Because we have become accustomed to the comforts brought about by science, we tend to lazily and casually overlook the heavily price we have to pay for them.

Consciousness is the spiritual quality of life.

The life observed within matter is coming from the souls; they belong to God's marginal energy, which has consciousness as one of its fundamental properties. The souls account for life. In other words, they animate the bodies made of material energy. So the presence of life within this world is not due to a random combination of chemical elements; neither has consciousness arisen by further random evolution as a development of living matter – two unproven assumptions. According to the *Vedas*, life is present in the universe from its very beginning with the first being born in it, the demigod Brahma, God's "minister" of creation, who created the different bodies which other souls come to occupy. Life is actually due to the presence of the souls, who have consciousness as a part of their inherent make up as I just mentioned. The symptom of the presence of the soul is life, and consciousness is the spiritual quality of life. It is nonphysical and eternal. It is not a part nor a product of material nature but a quality of the spiritual nature. The souls, who belong to that nature, have that quality. And they are not found only in human beings, as commonly misunderstood. It is not that we *have* a soul, rather every living being *is* a soul, an individual conscious spark of higher, spiritual energy, encased in a body made of inferior, material energy.

Science has so many new things to learn. New things and ideas are what we do not know and should remain open to, in spite of the human mind's inherent tendency to be conservative and resist the truth contained in contrary opinions, however self-evident they may be. Therefore, the scientific approach is not sufficient to gain a substantial understanding of truth, even material truths, what to speak of metaphysical truths, like the soul or God and the transcendental sphere. Why deny them *a priori* and proudly insist in the name of so-called rationalism that the only reality is matter? The Greek philosophers used reason too but not automatically with such a reductionist conclusion. Science is science, it is not atheistic nor theistic. The Egyptians and Babylonians knew a lot about the orbits of the heavenly bodies, for instance, which is a scientific topic, but they regarded them as religious secrets.

The atheistic scientists posit that they deal with reason and facts while religion is irrational and rests solely on blind sentimental faith; but this is a baseless assumption, an act of theological ignorance. In the Vedic tradition at least, religion has underlying, substantial and elaborate Aristotelian-like logic evidences. It is entirely reasonable faith. Since it can be argued that faith can make one justify whatever one has been trained or raised to believe, the Vedas do not encourage blind faith at all, but present spiritual truths with a built-in system of argumentation. The Vedic way to teach is dynamic. The Vedic teachers present a point, like a thesis, then propose an opposite point or antithesis with arguments to back it up; points are made from both angles, then a reconciliation or synthesis is made and the *siddhanta* (conclusive truth) is established. The *Vedanta-sutra*, for instance, is a philosophical text where this method is demonstrated in an amazing masterful manner. The *Bhagavad-gita* presents also spiritual teachings in the form of a dialogue between Shri Krishna, the original Spiritual Master, and Prince Arjuna, who is not only a greatly heroic warrior but a great spiritualist as well, asking questions on our behalf in order to dissipate our doubts. Vedic students are thus trained to attack their own philosophical position with arguments, arguing against their own belief so to speak, with possible doubts to test its value before accepting it, thus making their faith strong and reasoned. In other words, in the Vedic spiritual educational system, one is argued into his faith with many philosophical arguments, so only a very neophyte untrained student can be argued out of it. Usually, most of those who have only a faith-based religious belief are also not easily argued out of their religion, but for a different reason: it is because, since their religion is more a cultural inheritance from birth – which they imbibed along with all the general assumptions, values, paradigms, allegiances and behaviors of any given culture – than a personal deliberate chosen commitment, they were not argued into it to begin with, but slowly indoctrinated without the backing of reason, or ever so rarely. That is why Mahatma Gandhi suggested that one converts deliberately to his own inherited religion on the basis of reason, not just out of customary habit. For the same reason, the Danish philosopher Soren Kierkegaard (1813-1855) was firmly opposed to the baptism of infants, arguing that the first Christians were all adults who converted willfully. To believe just out of faith without the backing of reason is therefore not the Vedic tradition, but is typical of the three Semitic religions. If those believers were submitting their own faith to the same brutal examination of the evidence and arguments that they use when they are approaching the teachings and beliefs of other religions, as suggested by John W. Loftus with his OTF or Outsider Test of Faith,[128] many if not most of them would probably be in for a big surprise and would have to reconsider

---

[128] *The Christian Delusion, Why faith Fails,* Prometheus books, NY, 2010

many dogmas they have been raised with or have accepted blindly without deep analysis. But let us not be naïve, as people just believe what they want to believe. Many people accept relativist or atheistic positions without evidence just because they feel more comfortable. Religious believers may do exactly the same. A Christian basking in the delusional belief that he is "saved" simply by having faith that Jesus gave his life as a vicarious atonement for his sins, may not want to budge from that position no matter what argument or evidence you present to him that the Bible cannot be God's word as it contains so many inconsistencies and that the self-appointed apostle Paul concocted the core beliefs of the Christian faith.

Actually, aren't real science and religion parallel endeavors ultimately in search of the same thing: the meaning, purpose and origin of life? Why divorce science from the religious dimension? Why not incorporate spiritual principles in the scientific works? Can't there be unity in diversity? Can't they converge, interact with an open mind, influence and inform each other? The believers in modern atheistic science are just like the religious believers that they criticize. They accept unproven assumptions exactly like them. They should test their faith in science from the point of view of a critical outsider. There are unsubstantiated philosophical assumptions and theories disguised as science, born from preconceived materialistic ideas, such as Darwinian spontaneous generation, macroevolution and natural selection, which are nothing but Bad Science (B.S.). To present as scientific truths these concocted theories which remain up-to-date unproven is nothing short from cheating. Who is naïve enough to believe the fable that a living organism, like the body of an animal or of a human being, with all its organs and different systems, can be the product of random, blind, automatic evolution? Such a tale is not science but a belief. And how could such organism have lived during the alleged successive transitional stages of its existence, when an organ or a system was being developed and was therefore not functional?

Mathematic calculations about the possibility of the eye with its amazing complexity having evolved by chance show at least 10 billion to one against, and perhaps many orders of magnitude greater than that.[129] For instance, if we were to transpose on the ground the work done just by the liver, it would require various factories occupying acres! Are we to believe that it was produced by chance? Macroevolution, or the transforming of one species into another one, is another unproven theory worthy of joining others on the garbage pile. Only microevolution (minor changes within the same species) has ever been observed. The so-called scientists argue, *"But it took millions and millions of years to happen in the past so give us some more time to demonstrate it in the present."* Again, this is not science but wishful assumption. Sorry, we do not accept such "postdated check". Is it reasonable to think that the conditions for life to happen on our planet are so perfect but it all happened by chance and for no reason, and all one can hope for is not to suffer too much and enjoy as much as possible whatever little pleasure one can squeeze out of matter before to enter into eternal naught? All this huge universe with such a complexity and endless variety would be meaningless? Science is dependent on some worldview or philosophy. Thus it can be seen that theistic scientists find through their observations yet another confirmation of their faith in God. Meanwhile, atheistic scientists see the same evidence but they have ruled out an intelligent cause; therefore, they refuse to let their observations go against their presupposed conclusions, based on their philosophical commitment to materialism. Thus they claim and try to prove that God does not exist, saying things like, *"Although it looks like it has been designed for a purpose..."*, *"Although the random appearance of life would be indistinguishable from a miracle..."*, *"We cannot allow God to put a foot in the door..."* Contrary to inane theories, material energy is inert and unconscious. Molecules lack inherent purposes and

---

[129] Wysong, 1976, p.308

meaning. Such theories reduce life to utter meaninglessness and generate a sense of emptiness, hopelessness and unhappiness in a person's mind. Charles Darwin confessed in his autobiography that his theories had made him lose all higher aesthetic tastes, and thereby happiness, and that his mind seemed to have become a kind of machine made for grinding laws. Matter on its own has "low information content" in contrast with living organisms who have "high information content". It does not have a spontaneous capacity for self-organization, nor independent desire and purpose. As soon as we speak of organization, desire or purpose, we imply the existence of a personal, conscious, intelligent, resourceful entity.

Is God really a person?

Theistic scientists conceive that life and the universe have a meaning as well as a purpose, which are reflected in its structure and its way of functioning. We can observe in the natural world that there are precise laws, irreducible complexity, great organization and an extremely fine tuning and synchronizing of various interdependent parameters permitting life on earth: the more than one hundred (122) anthropic constants. All of this points to a purpose. So what are we to conclude? Doesn't an obvious design, both on the microcosmic and macrocosmic level, makes it legitimate to presume the existence at the origin of the world of an immensely powerful and intelligent cause, a designer, which means a person? This is called the Teleological Argument (from the Greek *telos*, design). One could object, "*This sounds like the God-of-the-gaps.*" Well, as the saying goes, if it looks like a duck, walks like a duck, quacks like a duck, no amount of wishful thinking nor voting will turn it into something else than a duck, will it? It is as simple as that. And that original cause possessing these personal attributes is the supreme being known as God. Again, this is natural, rational theology. The most powerful demigod, Brahma, described God when he was granted His audience and received from Him the power and knowledge to create, or rather to organize material energy according to His direction. Just like you get a user's manual when you purchase some machine, it is said that Brahma received Vedic knowledge from God at the time of creation as the user's manual for the great machine this universe represents, and specifically for the human "machine". People imagine God's form to be this or that, or claim He has no form, but the description of God given by Brahma is scientific, experienced knowledge. Brahma's body is made of pure intelligence; he is the most intelligent being in our universe, and he declared God to be the Cause of all causes – *sarva-karana-karanam*. He described the stunningly beautiful form of Bhagavan Shri Krishna, the "All-Attractive One". This is recorded in the most ancient Vedic text called the *Brahma-samhita*. Moreover, God personally descends in the material world from time to time and displays uncommon activities, which are recorded in the Vedic *Puranas*. The Vedic literature[130] mentions another natural principle called *sat-karya-vada*: Since a cause can be perceived through its effects, its characteristics are visible in its effects. In other words, the cause possesses the same characteristics than the effect. So if we see personality and other personal characteristics in man – an effect – they must automatically exist in his cause – God. So, yes, God is a person. However, His corporeality is totally spiritual, not made of flesh and bones. He does not have a material perishable form. God is unpredictable. He cannot be limited by our human conceptions. He is inconceivable, but He kindly reveals Himself in the Vedic scriptures as well as when He descends on earth, so we can conceive Him. By the way, you cannot pigeonhole Him, so it is only an assumption that the God-designed and fine-tuned anthropic principles enable life just on one planet, ours. In our modern ignorance, we wonder and have doubts if there is even life, what to speak of rational life, on other planets; however, the Vedic literature contains amazingly detailed information about

---

[130] *Srimad Bhagavatam* 3: 26, 49

these various forms of life and Vedic culture is present on all the higher planets and some of the lower ones. Just like English is the international language, Sanskrit, the language in which the Vedas are written, is the interplanetary language, *deva-nagari*, the "language of the gods."

The "Multiverse"

In their refusal to accept the obvious truth – the existence of a superior supernatural Being who established the laws of physics to govern His lower energy and is the master of the souls as well – atheistic scientists have imagined the modern theory of multiple universes, without any scientific ability to test out if they exist. Although materialistic science has not been able to solve the puzzle of what makes the laws of physics, they postulate that those universes all have different such laws and only chance – yes, the Goddess Chance – has made it possible that in our universe these laws allowed life to emerge after billions of years of evolution of blind chemical reactions. The theory of multiple universes is confirmed by the Vedas, but not in that sense at all. They teach that there are indeed countless universes, each one ruled by the same divinely ordained mechanism or laws. How many universes are there? The Vedic texts compare ours to a tiny mustard seed within a bag of mustard seeds. There are not an unlimited number of them, but there is a lot of them! At the time of creation, each universe first manifests as a seed coming out of God in His gigantic feature of Maha-Vishnu. After creation, it expands, as understood by modern scientists. When it comes to its destined end, after a cycle of hundreds of trillions of years, Shiva, who is like God's "minister of destruction", annihilates everything. The universe then contracts. This is maybe what modern scientists call the "Big Crunch". Everything and everyone are absorbed back into Lord Maha-Vishnu. It all remains there for eons of time, until the next creation,[131] at the beginning of which the universes are coming again out of Lord Maha-Vishnu's

---

[131] In the Jewish *Midrash* on *Genesis, rabbah* 3, it is mentioned that there were many worlds which were created and destroyed before this one.

transcendental body. Again a soul occupies the post of Brahma as the first being appearing in each universe. Vedic knowledge is again revealed to each one of them. Once these Brahmas have organized matter, the other souls incarnate in various bodies according to their past activities or *karma*. So the universe began due to an intelligent act of creation or – since from the Vedic point of view time is cyclical and material energy is eternal but is at times manifested and at times latent and not manifested – an act of re-manifestation of material energy by God, its eternal proprietor.

Even though they criticized or fought against the Church, besides a few exceptions, the philosophers of Renaissance and Enlightenment did not condemn Christianity or belief in God. Because they saw a natural and tolerant religion as useful to man, for them, atheism was even noxious and the atheists' fanatical refusal of any Divinity as dangerous for social cohesion as the Church.] [132] French philosopher Pierre Bayle (1647–1706) believed that even atheists could hold concepts of honor and go beyond their own self-interest to create and interact in society. Voltaire, on the other hand, held that without belief in a God who punishes evil, the moral order of society was undermined. He reasoned that since atheists, *"who are mostly bold and bewildered scientists who reason poorly."* gave themselves to no Supreme Authority and no law and had no fear of eternal consequences, they were far more likely to disrupt society. John Locke concurred and said that if there were no God and no divine law, the result would be moral anarchy: *"Every individual could have no law but his own will, no end but himself. He would be a god to himself, and the satisfaction of his own will the sole measure and end of all his actions"*. He did not hesitate to exclude them from the sphere of the tolerable *"because if you banish from the world the belief in God and deny His existence, you can only introduce chaos and confusion; the promises, contracts and good faith which*

---

[132] Frédéric Lenoir, *Le Christ philosophe*, Plon, 2007

are the main ties of civil society cannot motivate an atheist to keep his word."

Like for many reform movements which start with legitimate intentions, there was unfortunately a gradual radicalization and degradation of humanism. Truly, Christianity had failed its mission of enlightening people with a living example of Yeshua' teachings; it was therefore normal that it came under attack. [Soren Kierkegaard, a fervent Christian, denounced the whole ecclesiastical institution and thought that what had perverted Christianity was its promotion to the position of official religion of the Roman Empire. Since then, according to him, Christianity, that is the European society which had become Christian under the iron hand of the Church, had only turned its back to Jesus' reformatory and revolutionary message of emancipation from the weight of the group, tradition and organized religion and of personal freedom of choice. The institution had completely subverted his message and negated this inner freedom in order to safeguard the interests of the group and of tradition, and real Christianity had been totally altered. He denounced official Christianity as *"a crime, an illusion, a forgery, a tasteless watered down beverage and a revolting travesty. Because it maintained the illusion that its discourse and practices were Christian, whereas they were not, the Church made real Christianity inaccessible to people, keeping it hidden. This cheating suppressed real Christianity by favoring the expansion of a counterfeit version in a fraudulent way. Jesus' message is very intensely demanding. It compels man to stand up on his own two feet. The whole false Christianity is just an effort of man to fall back on his four to get rid of real Christianity. Since only courageous, lucid and determined individuals are able to put into practice the highly demanding message of the Gospel, it is useless and even dangerous to try to convert the masses. What has perverted the original message is its too rapid propagation, those millions of people with the label 'Christian', the number of whom is hiding the absence of real Christians and the unreality of Christianity"*][133]

Granted, official Christianity is discredited. Being a syncretism, not an authorized faith, it simply does not work. History is the proof and the judge. So Jesus and Christianity should be dissociated. Has Christianity made the world a better place? But is it the goal of religion to make the world a better place? Or isn't it rather to connect man with God and teach him to strive to reestablish one's forgotten relationship with Him and join Him in His eternal abode, forgetting this world? But following religious principles can and certainly will make life in this world better, maybe not the world itself, which suffers from "chronic imperfections".

One's religious commitment should be both reason-based and faith-based. Reason is too weak alone but can help, and faith without reason can be blind, sentimental or fanatical. But why give up faith in God altogether? If you realize that your faith does not rest on solid grounds, question it, and then give it up for a better, more solid one if you dare and are able to. I know that it is difficult, because when their faith is proven to them to be probably not genuine, Christians usually will not give it up but will kind of reinvent it, making some compromise. I think they do so because Christianity has been mostly preached with the element of fear and they are thus afraid to go to hell if they do not believe in it anymore, or because, due to the paucity of philosophy in the Christian faith, they are usually so sentimental or fanatical that as J. Loftus wrote, *"You must prove it to be impossible before they'll consider it improbable."* It seems that when it is shown to them to be impossible, or improbable, they only hear the last part of the sentence 'possible' or 'probable' and cling to it. Anyway, you may have to adjust and make big changes in your religious life and I know it is not easy, but do not

---

[133] idem

give up faith in God Himself. Do not do like John Loftus and others and throw the baby along with the bath water. Atheism is not a proper alternative to disillusionment about your faith. That Yeshua is not God and that Christianity is a delusion is not equivalent to God not existing. I was born and raised in a Christian family and even went to the Catholic Seminary to become a priest. I understood Jesus is not God almost 50 years ago. That did not turn me into an atheist. If you do not believe in Yeshua as God any longer, please do not think of God as semi-impersonal and unknowable, or distant and terrible as He has been presented in the three Semitic religions. Please study the Vedic literature. Take up meditation, especially mantra-yoga, which is very simple but very powerful.

The Vedic origin of Yeshua's teachings

Where was what Jesus taught coming from? He was not just teaching traditional Jewish wisdom from the Bible. For instance, the concept of forgiving one's enemies and loving them is totally foreign to Judaism. On the other hand, it is found in the Vedic *Srimad Bhagavatam* (7th canto) and the *Bhagavad-gita* teaches equanimity towards friends and foes alike. Joseph Atwill argues that Jesus' teaching about loving one's enemies is the worst part of his teachings because it takes away humanity from his religion. But the point is that he was not creating a religion but enunciating very high spiritual principles that, truly, people on a regular religious level cannot follow; one has to be an advanced spiritualist having reached a high level and realized his-so called enemy is a soul like him, servant of the same God than him, as we saw earlier. Some people say that his teachings were coming from Buddhism or Stoicism. But these higher teachings are actually Vedic in nature. It is only much later that Buddhism, which has no theistic dimension nor deep transcendental teachings, has stressed the separate culture of the ancient Vedic values of detachment and compassion, which are in reality automatic byproducts of the cultivation of divine love. Stoicism has also Vedic roots, as many elements found in various Greek philosophers.

Made in the USA
Columbia, SC
27 October 2022